BRENDA KAY

oh So **Good**

Comfort Food
From a California Girl

TATE PUBLISHING
AND ENTERPRISES, LLC

Published by Tate Publishing & Enterprises, LLC
127 E. Trade Center Terrace | Mustang, Oklahoma 73064 USA
1.888.361.9473 | www.tatepublishing.com

Tate Publishing is committed to excellence in the publishing industry. The company reflects the philosophy established by the founders, based on Psalm 68:11,
"The Lord gave the word and great was the company of those who published it."

Book design copyright © 2012 by Tate Publishing, LLC. All rights reserved.
Cover design by Kenna Davis
Interior design by Blake Brasor

Published in the United States of America

ISBN: 978-1-61346-880-7
1. Cooking / Regional & Ethnic / American / Southern States
2. Cooking / General
12.07.10

Introduction

This is my story, a celebration of fifty years of real homemade cooking Southern style.

I'm a California girl but have always cooked Southern style. My family is from Missouri and Arkansas, so I grew up with Good Real Southern Home Cooking and am very proud of it.

I'm from a small town, Sanger, CA. I went to two grade schools in Sanger, Wilson, and Washington and then Sanger High School. When I finished high school, I got married to a wonderful man. I have two daughters, Staci and Shantal, and seven grandchildren. I am a widow. My husband passed away in December 2008. It was the biggest tragedy I've ever had to face, and I miss him very much.

In my recipes in the following pages, you'll find real Southern home cooking and baking tips and sweet memories of days gone by.

When I have family and guests over, I try to have a few samples of a little bit of everything. I've always had Southern hospitality and its distinctive preparation.

It is possible to make a lot of dishes that taste different even with the same ingredients. However, truly good cooking is when you are able to share the joy of cooking those delicious meals that anyone can prepare. I hope it will be a welcome addition to your present collection of recipes. In this book, you will find a wide variety ranging from traditional to the most innovative cooking ideas, just good ole down home cooking.

Best Cooking to All
—Brenda Kay

Table of Contents:

Equivalents:

3 tsp	. . . .	1 tbsp.
4 tbsp	. . . .	1/4 cup
5 1/3 tbsp	. . . .	1/3 cup
8 tbsp	. . . .	1/2 cup
10 2/3 tbsp	. . . .	2/3 cup
12 tbsp	. . . .	3/4 cup
16 tbsp	. . . .	1 cup
1/2 cup	. . . .	1 gill
2 cups	. . . .	1 pt.
4 cups	. . . .	1 qt.
4 qts	. . . .	1 gal.
8 qts	. . . .	1 peck
1 peck	. . . .	1 bu.
16 oz	. . . .	1 lb
32 oz	. . . .	1 qt.
8 oz. liquid	. . . .	1 cup
1 oz. liquid	. . . .	1 tbsp.

For liquid and dry measurements, use standard measuring spoons and cups. All measurements are level.

Helpful Information:

Fruits: 3 1/2 oz. = approximately 1/2 cup

Bread: 2/3 oz. = 1 thin slice

Butter: 1/6 oz. = 1/2 pt.

Milk: 7 oz. = 1 glass

Measuring:

All measurements in this book are level. You will be most successful if ingredients are measured accurately.

1. Flour: When recipe calls for sifted flour, sift before measuring. Spoon flour lightly into the correct size measuring cup. Do not tap cup or pack down. Fill to overflowing and level off with spatula.
2. Sugar: Do not sift. Otherwise, use same method as for flour.
3. Brown Sugar: Pack into the correct-sized dry measuring cup just firmly enough for sugar to keep the shape of the cup when turned out.
4. Shortening: Pack into the correct-sized dry measuring cup and level off.
5. Liquids: Place standard liquid measuring cup on level surface. Pour liquid into cup to correct measurement.
6. Baking Powder, Salt, Spices: Use standard measuring spoons. Heap ingredients in spoon. Level off with spatula.

General Oven Chart:

Very Slow Oven 250-300°F

Slow Oven 300-325°F

Moderate Oven 325-375°F

Medium-Hot Oven 375-400°F

Hot Oven 400-450°F

Very Hot Oven 450-500°

Baking Powder Biscuits. . . . . .450°F 12-15 minutes

Muffins . . . . .400-425°F 20-35 minutes

Quick Breads .350°F 40-60 minutes

Yeast Breads .375-400°F 45-60 minutes

Yeast Rolls . . . . .400°F 15-20 minutes

Butter Loaf Cakes. . . . . .350°F 45-60 minutes

Butter Layer Cakes . . . . .350°-365°F 25-35 minutes

Cupcakes . . . . .375°F 20-25 minutes

Chiffon Cakes . . . . .325°F 60 minutes

Sponge Cakes . . . . .325°F 60 minutes

Angel Food Cakes. . . . . .325°F 60 minutes

Bar Cookies .350°F 25-30 minutes

Drop Cookies . . . . .350°-375°F 25-30 minutes

Refrigerator Cookies. . . . . .350°-400°F 8-12 minutes

Meringues. .350°F 12-20 minutes

Pie Shell . . . . .350°F 12 - 15 minutes

Filled Pies. .450°F 10 minutes then lower to 350°F 40 minutes

Beef Roasts .325°F Rare 18-20 minutes per lb.

Medium 22-25 minutes per lb.

Well Done 30 minutes per lb.

Chicken . . . . .325°-350°F 30 minutes per lb.

Duck. . . . . .325°-350°F 25 minutes per lb.

Fish Filets. .500°F 15-20 minutes per lb.

Goose. . . . . .325°-350°F 30 minutes per lb.

Ham . . . . .350°F 20 minutes per lb.

Lamb . . . . .300°-350°F 35 minutes per lb.

Meatloaf . . . . .375°F 60 minutes for a 2 lb. loaf

Pork Roast .350°F 40 minutes per lb.

Turkey . . . . .250°-325°F 15-25 minutes per lb.

Veal Roast .300°F 30 minutes per lb.

Venison. . . . . .350°F 20-25 minutes per lb.

Helpful Hints:

1. Wrap your scouring pad in a paper towel after use. The towel takes up the moisture and the pad doesn't rust.

2. If you spill something on the inside of your oven, sprinkle salt on it as soon as possible. Chances are you'll be able to lift it out easily after the oven cools.

3. Polish your silver with baking soda? It works and doesn't even scratch. Mix three parts soda to one part water, making a paste. Use a damp sponge or soft cloth, and rub each piece until clean. Rinse and buff.

4. To remove black marks on the floors made by shoes, cover stains with a light coat of shortening, lard, or margarine. Sprinkle with baking soda and wipe up with dampened sponge.

5. Place meatloaf on top of a slice of bacon while baking and the loaf won't stick to the pan.

6. Keep your summer salads cool and covered, out of direct sunlight. There is a visual tip-off to know when mayonnaise has gone bad. The oil separates. If your salad develops a shine or film on top, the mayonnaise has broken down. The salad, even if it tastes all right, should not be eaten.

7. To remove grease stains from your wooden cabinets, spray with an aerosol laundry starch. After it has dried, simply rub off the starch and stain with a soft cloth.

8. When you are baking layer cakes, put a pan of water on the bottom oven shelf. Cakes will bake more evenly and be heavenly moist.

9. To control the cabbage worms, sprinkle rye flour over and around the plants while they are covered with dew.

10. To rid the house of ants, mix equal parts powdered sugar and powdered borax. Sprinkle along baseboards and in corners.

11. To keep lint from clinging to blue jeans and corduroys, add 1/2 cup vinegar to each wash load.

12. Tape a small sponge on the inside of your garbage can cover and keep it saturated with a disinfectant. This will lessen odors and will also keep out insects.

13. For a steady heat to raise bread in the time required in most recipes, turn oven to 200 degrees. When temperature is reached, shut off oven and put bread in to rise.

The Joy of Cast-Iron Cooking:

I have always known the joy of cooking with cast iron. Just tradition is reason enough. This is the only cookware that I cook with. I have had my original set for over fifty years and would not cook with anything else.

A better reason for cooking with iron perhaps is the flavor it imparts to great Southern recipes. An iron skillet greased with bacon dripping and preheated in a hot oven almost fries the cornbread batter when it is first poured into the pan, making a crisp and crunchy crust on the bottom.

How to Season Your Cast-Iron Cookware:

Wash a new pot or pan with mild dishwashing soap and a stiff brush. Never use abrasives or steel wool.

Grease the inside of the utensil with vegetable oil or shortening. (Do not use salted fat, such as margarine or salted butter.) Also lightly grease the outside of the cookware, wiping away any excess. Do the same for cast-iron lids.

Place the greased cast-iron cookware in a 300° to 350°F oven and let it season for 30-40 minutes. Turn the oven off. Leave the utensil in the oven overnight or until cooled to room temperature.

Some cooks repeatedly oil the pot or pan and then fill it with potato peels before slow-cooking to temper the iron taste.

Before putting it away, oil after each cleaning.

Helpful Hints:

1. For perfect popcorn, melt butter-flavored shortening in the corn popper and then add the desired amount of kernels. The end result is amazing. Not only does the corn pop evenly into perfect fluffy popcorn, it also has a flavorful butter taste with no added cholesterol.

2. Are you tired of having lumpy soups and gravies? Tired of having to strain out those unwanted lumps? You can make them lump-free every time. Instead of flour, use dried instant potatoes. Now your soups and gravies will always be smooth and lump-free, and much tastier too.

3. Pesky fleas, ants, and other bugs are repelled by mint. Mint gives easily in most localities, so plant it around your house and use the leaves around in your kitchen cabinets. If your dog doesn't have a flea collar, rub your dog with mint leaves. The dog will also smell better.

4. Use a vegetable peeler to slice cheese from a brick. The thin slices spread easily and melt quickly in recipes. For a quick cheese sauce, simply place some of these extra-thin slices on top of a bowl of hot vegetables.

5. After handling garlic, rub your hands over an unpeeled potato. It will neutralize the odor.

6. Use muffin tins to bake your biscuits. It helps to make them crustier and higher.

7. To prevent a scum from forming on the top of refrigerated puddings, place transparent plastic wrap lightly over the top of dish. Don't let wrap touch the pudding. Peel off before serving.

8. Don't throw away the sweet pickle juice. Buy a can of beets, drain, and add to pickle juice for pickled beets. Or, if you have a large amount of sweet pickle juice, add cooked florets of cauliflower or cooked carrots.

9. Cook a green pepper with a boiled cabbage. The neighbors won't know what you are having for dinner.

Hints for Breakfast:

1. When making hash brown potatoes, use seasoned salt instead of regular salt. It makes a tremendous difference to the taste.

2. For perfectly shaped pancakes, use a meat baster to squeeze your batter onto the hot griddle.

3. To make nice, fluffy pancakes, heat the egg yolks and add to batter. Whip egg whites until stiff and fold into the batter. The results will be nice, fluffy pancakes.

4. Adding a little sugar to the batter of pancakes and waffles will make them brown more quickly.

5. For evenly rounded tops on nut breads and muffins, grease baking pans or muffin cups on the bottom and only 1/2 inch up the sides. Do this and your batter will cling to the sides of the pan instead of sliding back down.

6. For biscuits with softer sides, place them in a baking pan with sides barely touching. For firmer sides, leave space in between them.

7. To quickly use that frozen juice concentrate, simply mash it with a potato masher. No need to wait for it to thaw. A wire whip works also.

8. Transfer your jelly to a small, plastic squeeze bottle. No more messy, sticky jars or knives.

9. When making scrambled eggs, for each egg, add 1 tbsp. of sour cream and 1/4 tsp. dill weed. Delicious!

10. To determine whether an egg is fresh, immerse it in a pan of cool, slated water. If it sinks, it's fresh. If it rises to the surface, throw it away.

11. Add a few drops of vinegar or a little salt to the water when poaching eggs. It will help keep the egg whites from separating.

12. Scrambled eggs for a crowd. Add a pinch of baking powder and 2 tsp. of water per egg.

13. Minimize bacon shrinkage by running bacon underwater before frying. This reduces shrinkage by almost 50 percent.

The Table:

The clang of the dinner bell and the call to the table are more than a summons to eat. They are a call to experience family, food, and conversation, an invitation to a daily family reunion.

Most of us learned and lived our family histories at the table. We were raised at the table, disciplined, rewarded, encouraged, and comforted there. We learned who God was at the altar of the kitchen table by hearing our fathers repeat the blessings we would later learn and say. Family holidays were all celebrated at the table with seasonal feasts. We were honored with a seat at the head of the table and punished by being sent from the table. And in our mothers' eyes, our table manners portrayed just what manner of people we were.

The table is the center of home and family everywhere you go.

"All things are ready, come to the feast! Come, for the table now is spread; Ye famishing, ye weary. Come, and thou shalt be richly fed."

Our Good, Old-Fashioned Sweet Tea:

I have always made this, but now many people think this is something new. I always boiled the tea bags on the stove, hoping they didn't break open, and then filled the container with water plus the tea water on the stove and added sugar and stirred. But now a fancy word for it is sun tea.

6-8 tea bags

1 big glass pitcher of water

2 cups sugar (more to taste)

Boil tea bags on the stove in water or put out in the sun in the big glass container until the water is dark enough to your liking. Discard tea bags either way; if boiled, add water to pitcher, or if sun tea, add the sugar to each and stir. Pour it in a glass of ice and you have sweet tea.

Hints for Appetizers and Dips:

1. Save leftover fruit juices until there's enough to freeze in an ice tray. The cubes add extra flavor to lemonade, iced tea, or Jell-O.

2. Drink jasmine tea or the lighter-bodied varieties like *formosa oolong*, which have their own natural sweetness. They are fine for sugarless iced tea too.

3. Calorie-free club soda adds sparkle to iced fruit juices, makes them go further, and reduces calories per portion.

4. When possible, float blocks of ice in punch rather than ice cubes. This not only is more decorative but also slows melting and diluting.

5. Try placing fresh or dried mint in the bottom of hot chocolate for a zesty taste.

6. Thaw frozen orange juice right in the container. Remove the top metal lid and place the opened container in the microwave. Heat on high power 30 seconds for 6 oz. and 45 seconds for 12 oz.

7. Never boil coffee. It brings out the acid and causes a bitter taste. Store coffee in the refrigerator or freezer to retain the fresh flavor.

8. Use a teaspoon of nonfat dry milk in your coffee or tea rather than nondairy creamers that contain saturated fats and sugar.

9. To keep tea and tea bags fresh, store them in an air-tight container in a cool, dark place away from strongly flavored foods.

10. When serving *hor d'oeuvres* on a silver tray, you might wish to protect the tray from acids by covering it with a layer of green lettuce.

11. Use yogurt instead of sour cream for dips and you will reduce the calorie content.

12. Buy a loaf of unsliced pumpernickel bread and freeze it for an hour so that you can slice it wafer thin. Then spread with unsalted butter and a light sprinkling of parmesan cheese. Toast at 325°F until crisp.

13. Cut circles of bread with a cookie cutter, spread with mayonnaise, and top with a cucumber and a pimento sliver or a sprig of dill.

Crisp Cheese Snacks:

Appetizers or snacks:

3 cups cheddar cheese (grated)

3 cups fine, sifted flour

2 tsp. vegetable oil

1 tsp. salt

1/4 cup corn starch

4 tbsp melted butter

3/4 cup cold water

Using a fork, mix salt, water, flour, and oil into a dough ball; dampen a cloth and put over dough in bowl; and let stand for at least one hour.

Roll the dough and cut into 4 pieces, and then roll each piece as thin as possible.

Sprinkle the grated cheddar on each of the four sections. Then fold each section closed, pinching the edges closed and cutting into four more strips.

Place a buttered baking dish and cover with melted butter.

Bake at 350°F for 25 minutes or until golden brown.

Fresh Mushroom Cutlets:

These are easy but must be made at the very last moment:

1 cup finely chopped mushrooms

1 green onion, minced

2 eggs

1/2 cup breadcrumbs

3/4 cup grated mild cheddar cheese

Salt (to taste)

Pepper (to taste)

Mix all ingredients well, but do not turn into a mush. Pinch off about a teaspoon of mix and sauté in a little bit of butter until done. Taste and adjust seasoning if necessary.

Form remaining mix into eight patties about 3/4 inch thick and press into shape between sheets of waxed paper. Fry patties in butter over low heat. The outside of the cutlet should be crisp, and the inside should be moist.

Serve plain or melt a slice of cheese over each cutlet before serving.

Fresh Fried Mushrooms:

I needed something to go with hamburgers one night for dinner, and I said, "Why not see what these will taste like?" So I mixed the batter together, and it was great:

1 lb medium-sized fresh mushrooms

1 egg beaten

1/3 cup milk (a little more if needed)

1 cup flour

Salt to taste

Trim fresh mushrooms and wipe with a damp paper towel. Mix egg and milk together. Dip mushrooms into mixture and then into flour. Fry in hot, deep oil until golden brown. Drain on paper towel. Salt to taste after they come out of the fryer.

Cheese Balls:

1/2 lb sharp cheddar cheese

6 3-oz. packages cream cheese

2 tsp. grated onion

1 tsp. Worcestershire sauce

1 clove garlic, crushed (or finely minced)

2 oz. finely chopped pecans or walnuts

Grate the cheddar cheese and combine with softened cream cheese, preferably with electric mixer. If too stiff to blend well, add a little cream or milk. Add grated onion, Worcestershire sauce, and garlic. Mix well. Butter a mold (any shape) heavily and sprinkle the chopped nuts all over inside the mold. Then carefully pour the cheese mixture into mold. Chill for several hours (better if made a day ahead) and serve with crisp crackers. Turn over and lift out very gently.

Goody! Stuffed Mushrooms:

18 regular whole mushrooms

3 tbsp. butter

1 onion, chopped

1/2 tsp. salt

1/2 tsp pepper

2 tbsp. chopped parsley

2 tbsp. water

Remove stems from mushrooms and chop coarsely. Sauté in butter with onions. Add water, seasonings, parsley. Add to cream sauce. Fill mushroom caps. Top with buttered crumbs.

Bake at 350°F for 15 minutes.

Hints for Soups, Stews, and Sandwiches:

1. You can use instant potatoes instead of flour to thicken soups, stews, and gravies without lumps. Another excellent thickener for soup is a little oatmeal. It will add flavor and richness to almost any soup.

2. If soup has been oversalted, add a teaspoonful of sugar or a few small pieces of raw turnip and simmer a little longer. This will neutralize the salt flavor.

3. Grate a raw potato and add it to your soup when it is too salty. Or add a whole raw potato and remove it before serving. The potato absorbs the salt.

4. All seasonings should be added gradually to soup or the flavor might be too strong.

5. A little finely grated cheese added to thin soup improves the taste immensely.

6. Remember, soup boiled is soup spoiled. Soup should be cooked gently and evenly.

7. To prevent curdling of milk or cream in soup, add the soup to the milk rather than vice versa. Or add a bit of flour to the milk and beat well before combining.

8. Cream soups tend to boil over easily. Some cooks say that greasing the top edges of the cooling container will prevent this problem. One quart of soup yields about six servings, unless it is the main course.

9. To save money and add vitamins, pour all leftover vegetables and cooking water into a freezer container. When the container is full, add tomato juice and

seasoning. Use the contents for making nutritious soups, stews, or casseroles. Or try freezing the vegetables and water separately, and use the water in place of chicken or beef broth.

10. Vegetables added to soup will make a much tastier dish if you sauté them first, preferably in a little butter.

11. A leaf of lettuce dropped into the pot absorbs the grease from the top of the soup. Remove the lettuce and throw it away as soon as it has served its purpose. Or float a piece of tissue paper lightly on top of the soup and it will absorb the grease.

12. Fat can be skimmed off soup by chilling soup until fat hardens. If time does not permit this, wrap ice in a paper towel and skim over the top.

13. Steak, roast, or poultry bones can be frozen until needed for soup stock.

14. Always start cooking bones and meat in cold, salted water.

15. Instant soup stock will always be on hand if you save the pan juice from cooking meats. Pour the liquid into ice cube trays and freeze. Place solid cubes in freezer bags or foil.

Old-Time Oyster Soup:

I remember this so well when I was a child. Put in a bowl when done and load it with broken crackers and pepper. There is nothing much better.:

Milk (halfway full in medium-sized pan)

1 8-oz. can whole oysters (juice and all)

3-4 tsp. butter, cubed

pepper (to taste)

Pinch of salt

Saltine crackers

Open can of oysters. Put in pan. Chop with knife until they are bite-sized pieces. Add milk and butter. I add pepper and salt while cooking. Cook until boiling. Be careful. It will boil over fast and make a big mess.

Serve in bowls. I put a lot of crackers in mine and more pepper. The crackers will soak a lot of it up, but that is the way I like it.

Hearty Meatball Soup:

Breadsticks and a crisp salad with dressing of your choice go perfectly with this meal. This soup is so good:

4 cups very hot water

1 (2.7-oz.) box Swiss tomato with basil soup mix

3 vegetable bouillon cubes

1 16-oz. can small, whole, white potatoes, drained

1 lb. lean ground beef

1 tsp. garlic powder

1 14 ½-oz. can stewed tomatoes (with juice)

1 12-oz. can Mexican-style corn, drained

1 10-oz. package frozen lima beans

1/2 tsp. dried thyme leaves

1/4 tsp. pepper

Salt to taste

Put water, soup mix, and bouillon in a 4-5-quart pot over high heat. Cover and bring to a boil, stirring occasionally. Meanwhile, quarter potatoes and add to boiling liquid with remaining ingredients except beef and garlic. Combine beef with garlic powder. Mix well. When soup returns to a boil, reduce heat so soup simmers. Push heaping tablespoons of beef mixture off spoon into soup. (You will get about 16 loosely shaped meatballs.) Simmer for 6-8 minutes until the meatballs are firm and no longer pink inside.

Makes 4 generous servings.

My Good Old Fried Egg Sandwich:

I never ate an egg sandwich until I married my husband, and they are the best:

1 skillet for frying

1-2 tablespoons shortening

2 eggs

2 slices white bread

1 slice American cheese

Mayonnaise

Salt (to taste)

Pepper (to taste)

Melt shortening in the skillet, break open egg, break the yellow, fry one side and then the other. When you turn it over, fry a little and then put a piece of cheese on top and fry until cheese is melted. Put mayonnaise on one slice of bread and add the one egg and then cook another egg without cheese. Cook both like a fried hard egg, making sure the yellow is cooked good and hard. When the second egg is done, put it on top of the first egg with the bread. Put mayonnaise on the second piece of bread and put it on top of both eggs and eat.

Asparagus Sandwich Puff:

6 slices of bread, toasted (buttered)

1 cup flaked tuna

6 slices pimento cheese (your choice)

1 lb asparagus, cooked

1/2 teaspoon salt

dash pepper

1 tbsp. salad dressing (your choice)

Spread toast with butter. Spoon tuna over toast and top with a slice of cheese. Add 4 asparagus spears per sandwich.

Beat egg yolks until thick and lemon colored. Add salt, pepper, and salad dressing. Beat egg whites stiff and almost dry, and then fold into yolk mixture. Spoon egg mixture over asparagus and bake on a cookie sheet at 350 degrees for about 15 minutes or until golden brown.

Makes 6 sandwiches.

Fantastic Minestrone Soup:

1 cup dried navy beans

1/4 lb. salt pork

1 clove garlic, minced

2 tbsp. chopped parsley

2 medium onions, sliced thin

3 leeks, white part, chopped

1 1/2 qt. water

1 1/2 can diced tomatoes

1 1/2 cup chopped celery

6 carrots, chopped

1 green pepper, chopped

1 tbsp. salt

1 tsp. basil

1/8 tsp. black pepper

1 1/2 cup shredded cabbage

1 cup peas

1 cup lima beans

1/2 cup cooked macaroni

Soak dried navy beans overnight in 1 qt. water. Add cut pork, put garlic, parsley, onions, and leeks. Cook 10 minutes more. Add the beans and the water in which they were soaked. Then add water, tomatoes, celery, carrots, green pepper, salt, basil, and black pepper. Simmer 2 hours.

Add cabbage, peas, and lima beans and simmer 15 minutes.
Add the macaroni. Cook macaroni until it is tender in the soup.
Serve hot with parmesan cheese sprinkled on top.
This is best when made the day before the party.
Serves 8.

Good Old Clam Chowder:

My children just love this soup. Myself, I'm not a fish person, but once in a while is okay:

6 slices bacon

1 cup diced sweet onion

2 8-oz. cans minced clams

1 8-oz. bottle clam juice

3 cups diced potatoes

4 tbsp. flour

3 cups light cream

1 tsp. salt

Pepper to taste

1 cup milk

In large saucepan or Dutch oven, gently fry bacon until crisp. Add bacon, onion, and fry until deep golden brown. Remove with slotted spoon. Add liquid drained from clams, bottled clam juice, and potatoes to pan drippings. Cover and boil gently until potatoes are tender. With wire whisk, gradually stir one cup of cream into flour. Add to potato broth mixture with remaining cream, drained clams, and salt and pepper. Cook over moderately low heat, stirring constantly until thickened. Stir in milk and crumbled bacon. Heat but do not boil.

4-6 servings.

Beef Stew:

1 tsp. salt

1/2 tsp. paprika

1/4 cup flour

2 tbsp. fat

2 cups water

2 tbsp. catsup

6 medium potatoes, peeled

6 medium carrots, peeled

4 medium onions, chopped

1 tsp. pepper

!/2 half boneless beef stew meat

Cube meat into small pieces, roll in seasoned flour, and brown in fat in heavy kettle. Make sure every piece is well browned for best flavor. Add 2 cups water and simmer in tightly covered kettle until meat is tender, about two hours. Then add vegetables that have been cut into fairly large chunks and continue cooking in covered kettle until vegetables are tender. Add three table-spoons catsup, salt, and pepper to taste and just a little flour to thicken if broth is too soupy. (Mix flour and cold water before adding.) Serve while steaming hot.

Hints for Breads and Spreads:

1. Dry yeast is soaked or softened in warm liquid. Technically, you cannot dissolve the yeast; it is a living organism, cells merely separate, active, and reconstitute to expand and reproduce. They will appear to dissolve only because the cells are exceedingly small.

2. How water kills yeast. You can tell if the temperature is correct by pouring the water over your forearm. The water should be lukewarm or room temperature—neither hot nor cold.

3. Add 1/2 tsp. of sugar to the yeast when stirring it into the water to soften. If it foams and bubbles in ten minutes, you know the yeast is alive and active.

4. There is a difference in the yeast called for in old recipes and today's recipes. A cup of yeast called for in some older recipes is similar to sourdough batter; 2 ounces yeast called for in a 1954 cookbook is equal to one-fourth ounce envelope of today's yeast.

5. Use water that has been used to boil potatoes to make bread more moist. It adds flavor and provides food for the yeast.

6. When milk is used in making bread, you get a finer texture. Water makes a coarser bread.

7. When creaming butter and sugar together, it's a good idea to rinse the bowl with boiling water first. They'll cream better.

8. Dough won't stick to your hands if it is kneaded inside a large plastic bag.

9. To help yeast dough rise quickly and evenly, use a heating pad. Set the covered bowl on the pad with its temperature set at medium. If the television is in use, set the bowl on top. It makes a nice, warm spot for dough to rise.

10. Another way to raise bread is turn the oven to 200 degrees. When temperature is reached, shut oven off and put bread in to rise.

11. Dough can be risen in 15 minutes using a microwave. Place the dough in a microwave-proof bowl and put it in microwave with another container of 8 ounces of water. Heat at 10 percent power (or lowest setting) for 3 minutes. Let rest in the oven for 3 minutes, then heat again for 3 minutes. Let rest 6 minutes. Dough should have doubled in bulk and is ready for shaping.

12. To thaw frozen bread loaves, place in clean brown paper and put in a 325 degree oven for 5 to 6 minutes to thaw completely. For thawing rolls, allow several more minutes. Twenty seconds in the microwave is enough time for 2 slices to thaw.

13. Use shortening, not butter or oil, to grease pans, especially for bread, as butter and oil are absorbed more readily into the dough or batter and do not help release baked goods from pan.

Cheese Muffins:

1 cup grated American cheese

1 egg

2 cups sifted flour

3 tbsp. melted cooled shortening

3 tsp. baking powder

1 cup milk

1 tsp. salt

Sift the flour with baking powder and salt, and then mix with 3/4 cup of the cheese. Mix the egg, shortening, and milk together in separate bowl, and then stir into the cheese mixture with a fork.

Spoon about 2/3 full into greased muffin pans and sprinkle the remaining cheese on top of each one.

Bake in 425 degree oven for 25 minutes until brown.

Cinnamon Raisin Sour Cream Muffins:

1 1/2 cups flour

1 1/2 tsp. baking powder

1/2 tsp. baking soda

1/4 cup (1/2 stick) butter, melted

2 tbsp. sugar

1/4 cup milk

1 tsp. ground cinnamon

1/4 cup raisins

1/4 cup sour cream

1 egg

Heat oven to 400°F.

Mix flour, baking powder, and baking soda in a large bowl. Mix until mixture resembles coarse crumbs. Make a well in center of mixture.

Beat egg in a small bowl. Add sour cream, sugar, cinnamon, raisins, butter, milk. Add to flour mixture, mixing just until moistened.

Spoon into greased muffin pan, filling each cup 1/2 full. Bake 15 minutes or until lightly browned. Makes 12 muffins.

Missouri Cornbread:

My husband always loves cornbread. He has to crumble it up in a big glass of cold milk. Boy, it doesn't get much better:

> 2 eggs (separate)
>
> 2 tsp. sugar
>
> 3 tsp. baking powder
>
> 1 cup cornmeal
>
> 1 cup milk
>
> 1 cup flour
>
> 2 tbsp. butter (melted)
>
> Pinch of salt

To the yolks, add the sugar and beat well. Then add the cornmeal, milk, flour, melted butter, beaten egg whites, baking powder, and salt. Mix well.

Pour into greased 9x13-inch glass baking dish.

Bake in a preheated 400 degree oven until golden brown.

Cut into squares.

Good and Yummy Banana Nut Bread:

When I have over ripe bananas is when I usually make this bread. Just the smells from the kitchen when it is cooking is yummy:

1/2 cup butter (softened)

2 cups sugar

2 eggs

4 overripe bananas (mashed)

2 cups flour

1/2 tsp. baking soda

1/2 tsp. vanilla

1 cup chopped walnuts (More to taste. I like a lot in mine.)

Grease and flour 1 large or 2 small loaf pans.

In a large bowl, cream together the butter and sugar and add the eggs, blending well. Add the mashed bananas, flour, baking soda, vanilla, and nuts. Mix well.

Pour the batter into the prepared pan.

Bake in a preheated 300 degree oven for 1 hour or until golden brown.

Makes 1 large or 2 small loaves.

My Old-Fashioned Zucchini Bread:

My family loves this bread. It is so good with any meal. I like to eat it with butter spread on it:

Beat together:

3 eggs

2 cups grated zucchini

1 cup vegetable oil

2 cups sugar

Mix and add to the above:

2 cups flour

1 tsp. salt

2 tsp. soda

1/4 tsp. baking powder

2 tsp. cinnamon

1 1/2 cups nuts (walnuts)

3 tsp. vanilla

Bake at 350 degrees for about 60 minutes. Watch that it doesn't burn. Makes 2 loaves. (I make mine in a large glass low baking dish).

My Hot Roll Kalzonies:

Every time we went to an Italian restaurant, my husband would always want this dish, so I said, "I can make this," and I did:

   1 lb ground beef

   1 4-oz. can tomato paste

   Garlic salt to taste

   Grated Jack cheese

   1 package Pillsbury hot roll mix

Prepare hot roll mix according to directions on box. While dough is rising, brown ground beef and add tomato paste and garlic salt. Simmer for 2 minutes. Set aside and let cool.

When dough has doubled (30 minutes to 1 hour), divide into 12 balls. Roll balls out into round circles. Put spoonful of meat mixture in center, sprinkle cheese over meat, fold one side of dough over and then the other. Seal the edges. Roll up end and seal. However, you make the shape of the *kalzonie*, be sure you have sealed meat inside before frying.

Put cooking oil into skillet and heat. Fry *kalzonie* one or two at a time, on both sides. Make sure oil does not get too hot or dough will not have time to cook through before outside is brown. Drain on paper towels and serve.

Good Old Flour Biscuits:

As long as I can remember, my grandmother always had this mix stored in jars and cans in her cupboards. We had biscuits just about with every meal. You always had to use it up as fast as you could.

Biscuit Mix: For Storing

6 cups flour

1 tbsp. salt

1/4 cup sugar

3 tbsp. baking powder

1 cup Crisco shortening

Mix well, store in cool place

For 6 Biscuits:

1 cup mix

1/4 cup milk

For biscuits, mix well and turn on floured board. Knead lightly. Roll out and cut. I use a glass top part dipped in flour and then place cut-out biscuit on greased cookie sheet.

Bake at 400 degrees for 15 minutes or until golden brown.

My Good Old Yeast Buns:

I always make these on Thanksgiving and Christmas, and they are oh so good:

> 2 cups milk (warm)
>
> 1/2 cup sugar
>
> 1 tsp. salt
>
> 1 packet dry yeast
>
> 1 cup (soft) shortening
>
> 3 eggs (optional)
>
> 7 cups all-purpose flour

Dissolve the yeast packet in 1 cup warm water and 1 tbsp. sugar.

Scald milk and let cool. Add yeast mixture.

Add sugar, salt, shortening, and eggs. Beat well. Gradually add the flour and knead until smooth. Shape into balls the size of large eggs and flatten, and then let rise about 1 hour.

Bake at 375 degrees for about 25 to 30 minutes or until golden brown. Makes about 3 doz.en.

When adding the eggs, this recipe might also be used for sweet roll dough.

My Lemon Bread with a Twist:

2 cups sugar

4 eggs

1 cup milk

3 cups flour

2 tsp. baking powder

1 tsp. salt

Grating rind and juice from 2 lemons

3/4 cups sugar

1 cup shortening

Cream together shortening and 2 cups sugar. Add the rind of the two lemons. Add eggs, beating in one at a time. Add milk alternately with dry ingredients.

Bake at 350 ... 1 hour depending on you oven

While the bread is still hot and in the pans, punch holes in top with toothpick and pour over remaining sugar mixed with the juice from the lemons. Remove from pans when cool.

Makes 2 9x5x3-inch loaves.

Hush Puppies:

Just the thing for eatin' with fried fish:

2 cups cornmeal

1/2 cup water

1 1/2 cups milk

2 tsp. baking powder

1 tsp. salt

1 med. onion, diced

Olive oil

Mix all ingredients together and teaspoonfuls drop into hot oil. Fry until golden brown.

Goody Old Pancakes:

My family likes these a lot for dinner. Nice change:

  4 cups flour

  3 cups milk

  4 level tsp. baking powder

  1 tsp. salt

  4 tbsp. melted shortening

  2 eggs

Combine ingredients in mixing bowl. Beat until light. Spoon onto hot griddle. Cook until browned on each side. When done, cover with butter and pancake syrup.

Refrigerator Rolls:

2 packages cake yeast

1/4 cup lukewarm water

1 cup milk (scalded) like burning

1/2 cup light corn syrup

1 tbsp. salt

2 eggs

1/2 cup melted shortening

6 cups flour

Soften the yeast in lukewarm water. and add the syrup and salt. Add 2 cups of flour and beat well. Add the yeast. Beat the eggs in a separate bowl and add them. Blend well and add the shortening and remaining flour to make a soft dough. Knead until smooth and satiny. Place in a lightly greased bowl. Grease top of dough. Cover well and put into refrigerator and punch down. Mold at once in any desired shape or, if preferred, let the dough stand in a warm room for an hour before molding. Place the rolls in greased pans and let them rise until double in bulk.

Bake in moderately hot oven 375 degrees for 15 to 20 minutes.

Grandma's Easy-Do Rolls:

3 cups sifted flour

1 1/2 tsp. soda

3/4 tsp. salt

1 tbsp. sugar

1/3 cup shortening

1 package dry yeast

1/4 cup lukewarm water

6 tbsp. vinegar

Enough sweet milk to make 3/4 cup liquid

Sift flour, soda, salt, and sugar together and cut in shortening. Soften yeast in lukewarm water. Heat vinegar and milk to lukewarm and combine with yeast. Add liquid to dry ingredients gradually and stir only until flour is blended. Dough should be as soft as can be handled. Turn onto lightly floured board. Knead gently one minute. Shape as desired. Place on lightly greased baking pan. Let rise about an hour until doubled in size in warm place.

Bake at 400 degrees for about 15 minutes or golden brown.

Makes approximately 18 rolls.

Yummy Hot Rolls:

My family will eat them as bread during their meal and then turn right around and eat them with jelly for dessert:

Combine 2 packages yeast, 1 tsp. sugar, and 1 cup lukewarm water. Let stand for 10 minutes.

After 10 minutes, add:

1 cup warm water

6 tbsp. melted butter

5 tbsp. sugar

6 cups flour (or enough for a fairly stiff dough)

2 tsp. salt

Pour out on a floured dough board and knead well. Place dough in greased bowl covered with clean cloth and let rise in warm place until doubled in size. Then cut out, place on greased pan, and let rise until double in size again.

Bake in 400-degree oven until browned.

Country Biscuits:

Sometimes I will make these with our dinner at night or good old biscuits and gravy in the morning. These biscuits are darn good. I've been sittin' at my table seein' my biscuits disappear faster than a snow in August. Of course, I was right in there helpin' them vanish too:

In a bowl, sift the following dry ingredients:

4 level teaspoons baking powder

1 teaspoon salt

1 cup milk

2 tablespoons shortening

2 cup flour

Mix dry ingredients together, and then add the milk and enough flour to make a stiff batter. Pat out on floured board, cut in circles (I use a glass), and bake in very hot 400-degree oven.

Yum! Corn Fritters:

Here's a new wrinkle you might want to try 'bout corn pickin' time if the squirrels an coons didn't get the crop:

12 ears sweet corn

2 eggs,

1 cup flour

1 tsp. baking powder

1/2 cup milk

salt and pepper to taste

Remove corn from cobs. Combine corn with eggs beaten separately, flour, baking powder, and milk. Add salt and pepper to taste. Mix well and drop by spoonfuls in hot, deep fat. Turn and brown on both sides. Take out and drain.

Sizzling Hoe Cakes:

It is simple, quick, an' mighty tasty:

> 2 cups cornmeal
>
> 1/2 tsp. salt
>
> 1/2 tsp. baking powder
>
> 1 tbsp. melted fat

Combine 2 cups cornmeal and 1/2 tsp each of salt and baking powder. Add 1 tsp melted fat and stir in water to make a soft dough. Make into small cakes about half an inch thick, and bake on a hot, greased griddle or iron skillet (like a pancake) until brown and then turn to brown on other side:

Old-Fashioned Corn Bread:

We've sat down to many a mess of beans, onions, cold milk, an' corn bread from this very recipe. Mighty good with just about anything.

2 cups white meal (coarse ground)

1 cup flour

1 tbsp. sugar

1 cup sweet milk

4 tsp. baking powder

1 egg

1 tsp. salt

Combine all dry ingredients and then add egg and enough sweet milk to make thin batter. Pour in hot, well-greased glass flat baking dish.

Bake in a hot oven, 400°, until golden brown on top.

My Classic Egg Salad Sandwich:

Old-fashioned and oh so good:

4 hard boiled eggs, chopped

1/2 cup diced celery

1/4 cup chopped green bell pepper

1/4 cup mayonnaise

1/2 tsp. dry mustard

8 slices white or wheat bread toasted

Mix eggs, celery, bell pepper, mayonnaise, and mustard. Put mayonnaise on each slice of bread. Put egg mixture on 1 slice of bread and top with other slice.

Hints for Salads and Dressings:

1. To prevent a vegetable salad from becoming soggy when it has to stand for a few hours, place a saucer upside down on the bottom of the bowl before filling it with the salad. The moisture will run underneath and the salad will remain fresh and crisp.
2. Stuff a couple of paper towels in the plastic bag with onions or radishes and they will stay fresh longer.
3. Lettuce won't "rust" in the refrigerator if it is wrapped in paper towels.
4. If you have trouble getting a head of lettuce or some other vegetable into a plastic bag, grasp the lettuce through the bag, then pull the bag over the lettuce.
5. Peel onions under water and they will not irritate the eyes.
6. Rub some dry mustard on your hands after peeling onions and then wash as usual. You will find that all odors will be removed.
7. When celery loses its crispness, place it in cold water. Slice a raw potato and add it to the water. Let this stand for several hours. Remove the celery and it will be crisp again.
8. If parsley is washed with hot water instead of cold, it retains its flavor and is easier to chop.

9. Green pepper is an excellent source of vitamin C. Cut it in strips to serve as nibblers and add it to salads and sandwich fillings. Peppers might be blanched and filled with tuna, potato, or macaroni salad.

10. To reduce calorie intake, mix powdered salad dressings into plain low-fat yogurt instead of oil and sour cream, or add buttermilk, cottage cheese, or tomato juice to the dressing. (take out)

11. Bottled salad dressings might be loaded with saturated oil and preservative. Make your own by mixing 3 or 4 parts polyunsaturated vegetable oil, olive oil, yogurt, or buttermilk with 1 part vinegar or lemon juice and seasonings.

12. If you mix the oil and vinegar into a salad separately, add the oil first. If you reverse the order, the oil just slides off the wet leaves.

13. Old spice jars are perfect one-shot salad dressing containers to take along with a salad lunch.

14. Slice tomatoes vertically rather than horizontally. The slices will stay firmer in your salad and they'll help keep the salad dressing from getting watery.

15. If you soak onion rings in cold water for about an hour, they'll taste milder in your salad.

Chicken Salad:

This was my mother's old-fashioned chicken salad. She did not ground any of the ingredients as they do today. She just diced and chopped:

8 cups cooked chicken (diced)

1 1/2 cup pecans (diced)

1 1/2 cup white seedless grapes cut in half

2 tsp. sugar

1/2 tsp. salt

3/4 cup celery (chopped)

1 1/2 cup apples (diced)

1/2 cup pickles (chopped)

1/2 pt. mayonnaise or salad dressing

Mix all ingredients together and chill. Serve on top of lettuce.

The Best Pasta Salad:

My good neighbor and friend, Lucia Avila, gave me this delicious pasta salad:

2 cups small shell shape macaroni

1 cup Lil' Smoky sausages (cut into slices)

1 cup thin deli ham (chopped)

Lettuce (chopped)

1-2 tbsp. real mayonnaise

Pinch of salt and pepper (if any)

Mix together macaroni, sausages, ham, and mayonnaise. Then add your chopped lettuce at the last so you can taste the crunch and mix together.

Country Pea Salad:

Very good and different:

  1 box frozen peas 10 oz. (thawed)

  1 cup celery (chopped), more if desired

  6 green onions (chopped)

  1 jar of bacon bits (all of it)

  1 handful of salted peanuts

  1/2 cup mayonnaise

  1 whole pint sour cream

Mix all ingredients together. Serve as is or chill in the refrigerator.

Great Coleslaw:

1 bag of chopped coleslaw

1 chopped small apple (diced)

1 cup raisins

1/2 cup mayonnaise (or more to taste)

1-2 tbsp. sugar

1 grated carrot

Mix all ingredients together. The longer it sits in the refrigerator, the better when it soaks all the ingredients into the mayonnaise.

Mama's Macaroni Salad:

I grew up with my mama's macaroni salad, and I still make it and love it:

> 2 cups salad macaroni, (cooked) drained
>
> 10 eggs (hard boiled), chopped
>
> Yellow onions (chopped, desired amount)
>
> 2 tbsp. mayonnaise (more if needed)
>
> 1-2 tbsp. mustard (more if needed)
>
> 1-2 tomatoes (chopped)
>
> Salt (to taste)
>
> Pepper (to taste)

Combine macaroni, chopped eggs, onions (yellow and red), mayonnaise, mustard, tomatoes, and salt and pepper. It is best to add salt and pepper while the macaroni is cooking.

Mix well together all ingredients.

My Favorite Potato Salad:

I use five big potatoes or ten small, russet potatoes

10 hard-boiled eggs

Half red onion (chopped)

Pickle relish (to taste)

1 small can chopped olives (4 oz.)

Dijon mustard (2 tablespoons)

Mayonnaise (1 cup) could take more

Salt (to taste)

Pepper (to taste)

6 green onions (chopped)

Dice potatoes into bite-sized chunks. Boil for 10 minutes (no more). You do not want them mushy. Put in refrigerator all day to get them good and cold. Chop up eggs and set aside. In separate bowl, mix mayonnaise, Dijon mustard, green onions, pickle relish, red onions, salt, and pepper. Mix well. Add this mix and chopped eggs to potatoes. Mix well. If you need more of something, then add it to your taste. I always keep adding until I get the taste I want.

My Fruit Salad You'll Love:

1 large can (14 oz.) fruit cocktail

1 small can tropical fruit

2.5-oz. box instant French vanilla pudding

3-4 bananas sliced

1 cup sugar (optional)

1 cup chopped walnuts (save some for the top)

1-2 package of Dream Whip

Mix ingredients together, except the Dream Whip, part nuts included. Follow Dream Whip directions. Mix just a little in the salad, and spread the rest all over the top. Sprinkle the rest of the nuts on the top.

Finger Jell-O It's Great:

I made these for my children when they were little, and my mother made them for me. I like to put on top of my salad or just eat it alone:

1 cup sugar

1 cup cold water

4 cups hot water

4 pkg. Knox gelatin

3 pkg. (2.9-oz.) Jell-O (any flavor)

1 cup whipping cream

Mix sugar, Knox gelatin, and hot water. Add the Jell-O mix. Add cold water. Mix well. Add whipping cream and mix well. Put it in the refrigerator and let it set.

Cut into squares and serve.

My Bingo Cherry Salad:

A sure winner at a luncheon:

 2 3-oz. packages gelatin (any flavor)

 2 cups water

 1 20-oz. can crushed pineapple

 1 21-oz. can cherry pie filling

 1 8-oz. package cream cheese

 1/2 cup sugar

 1/2 cup sour cream

 1 tsp. vanilla

 1/2 cup chopped nuts

In a large bowl, combine the gelatin and hot water. Add the pineapple and cherry pie filling. Pour into an 8x10-inch glass dish. Chill until set.

Soften the cream cheese (I let mine set out overnight if I'm going to use it the next day) and mix well with the sugar. Blend in the sour cream and vanilla. Spread over the gelatin mixture. Sprinkle with nuts on top.

Serves 6.

Good Old Lemony and Orange Gelatin:

This is an easy and fast one you'll want all the time. I like a piece on top of my tossed green salad:

1 20-oz. can crushed pineapple

1 3-oz. box lemon gelatin

1 3-oz. box orange gelatin

2 cups boiling water

1 tablespoon vinegar

1/2 cup sugar

1 cup grated raw carrots

1/3 cup chopped walnuts

Drain and measure the juice from the pineapple. Add the water if necessary to make 2 cups. Set aside. Dissolve the lemon and orange gelatin in the boiling water—add the vinegar and the sugar—and reserved pineapple juice. Refrigerate for 30 minutes or until slightly thickened. Stir in pineapple, carrots, and walnuts.

Chill until set. Cut into squares.

Serves 6.

Hints for Vegetables and Side Dishes:

1. Put a tablespoon of butter or a few teaspoons of cooking oil in water when cooking rice, dried beans, and pasta to keep it from boiling over and sticking together.

2. Add a teaspoon of lemon juice to each quart of water used to cook rice. The grains will stay white and separated.

3. Pasta products tend to lose texture and become too soft when frozen and reheated.

4. A few drops of lemon juice in water while boiling potatoes will whiten them.

5. Potato skins will remain tender if you wrap them in aluminum foil to bake them. Foil margarine wrappers also work well.

6. To improve the flavor of potatoes, add a little sugar to the water in which they are boiled.

7. Potatoes will take on a slightly golden taste and appearance if sprinkled lightly with flour before frying.

8. A well-beaten white of egg added to mash potatoes will enhance the looks and taste of the dish.

9. Give mashed potatoes a beautiful whipped cream look by adding hot milk to them before you start mashing. One tablespoon of butter added before mashing also enhances the flavor.

10. If someone in the family is on a salt-free diet, try cooking a turnip with the boiled potatoes. It makes it taste as if salt has been added.

11. Sweet potatoes will not turn dark if put in salted water (5 teaspoons to one quart water) immediately after peeling.

12. If you add a little milk to water in which cauliflower is cooking, the cauliflower will remain attractively white. A bit of lemon juice or vinegar added to the cooking water also makes cauliflower keep its snowy white color.

13. Use greased muffin tins as molds when baking stuffed green peppers.

14. Green pepper might change the flavor in frozen casseroles. Clove, garlic, and pepper flavors get stronger when they are frozen while sage, onion, and salt get milder or fade.

Fried Green Tomatoes:

When the harvest is plentiful, serve some tomatoes before they ripen. They're tart and tasty when coated with cornmeal and flour and lightly fried. My husband just loved these. They are so good:

3 medium green tomatoes, cleaned

1 cup cornmeal

1 cup flour

Salt (to taste)

Pepper (to taste)

Vegetable oil or shortening for frying

Cut tomatoes into 1/2-inch slices. Stir cornmeal, flour, and desired amount of salt and pepper together in shallow pan. Coat tomatoes slices in mix. In a large iron skillet, heat 1/4-inch-deep oil over medium heat to 350 degrees. Fry on one side until golden brown, turn, and fry other side until golden brown. Drain on paper towels. Serve hot.

Makes 6 servings.

Batter Fried Onion Rings:

6 1/2 cups flour

1 can (12-oz.) beer, active or flat

3 very large yellow onions

1 quart vegetable oil

Combine flour and beer in a large bowl and blend thoroughly, using rotary beater. Cover. Allow batter to stand at room temperature for at least 3 hours. (If batter is too dry, add in some water.)

Twenty minutes before the batter is ready, preheat the oven to 200 degrees. Carefully peel the papery skins from the onions so that you do not cut into the outside onion layer. Cut onions into 1/4-inch-thick slices. Separate the slices into rings. Pour enough oil in deep fryer or kettle to come 2 inches up the side of pan.

Dip a few onion rings into the batter with a fork, and then carefully place them in the hot oil. Fry rings, turning them once or twice until they are an even golden brown. Drain on paper towel. To keep warm, place in the preheated oven.

Good Old Deviled Eggs:

My grandchildren love deviled eggs and can eat them morning, noon, and night:

   12 eggs, hard boiled

   Salt (to taste)

   Pepper (to taste)

   Good mayonnaise (as much as needed)

   Mustard (as much as needed)

Boil eggs in water. Once water starts to boil, put a lot of salt in the water. That will make them easier to peel. Put in cold water and let cool. Peel eggs and cut long ways. Take out yolk and put in separate bowl. Mash up with fork. Add mayonnaise, mustard, and salt and pepper and mix well. Add filling to each half egg. Be sure not to make the mixture too runny with the mayonnaise because it will all run out of the egg. Make the mix firm.

Good Old Fried Okra:

I never liked okra until I tasted the way my husband's mother fixed it, and I'm sure you will too:

Cut up fresh okra into thin chunks

1/4 cup milk

1/4 cup flour

1/4 cup cornmeal

Salt (to taste)

Pepper (to taste)

1 egg

Vegetable oil for frying

Pour milk over cut-up okra. Let sit so it soaks good. Maybe 10 minutes. Add flour and cornmeal to okra. Add salt and pepper and egg. Mix all well until coated.

Fry in hot vegetable oil. Keep turning over until all is crispy.

Big Pot of Black-Eyed Peas:

So good right out of the pot:

2 cups black-eyed peas

Yellow onion (amount desired)

Butter (2-3 pats)

Salt (to taste)

Pepper (to taste)

Cook peas in a big pot with water covering the peas. You will have to add more water as they cook down if desired. Fry onion just a little to brown in the oil. Drain, add to peas, and salt and pepper to taste. Cook slowly on low heat so peas stay firm and don't break apart. Peas are done when soft and firm.

My Chili Beans:

These I could eat every day. I usually make a big pot just to have leftovers with mashed potatoes:

2 cups pinto beans

1 lb. ground beef

Yellow onion (chopped)

Beef chorizo (1 stick)

Johnson's chili (16 oz.-tub) (this is a chili brick)

Garlic powder (to taste) (I like a lot)

Salt (to taste)

Pepper (to taste)

Cook beans in a big pot with water covering beans. You might need to add more water, as they will cook down. When beans start to boil, add salt, pepper, and garlic powder and cook ground beef and onions in separate skillet in a little oil, chopping often until pink color is gone. Drain. Add meat to beans. Add chorizo and chili brick. Let heat good together.

Sweet Corn Griddle Cakes:

1 pint of grated corn (off the cob)

1 cup flour

1 tablespoon melted butter

4 eggs

1 teaspoon salt

1 teaspoon baking powder

Milk (to the thickness of batter you desire)

Combine corn, flour, melted butter, eggs, salt, and baking powder with enough milk to make a batter of the right consistency. Cook on hot griddle or hot oil in a cast iron skillet.

Pan-Fried Corn:

2 cups tender yellow corn cut from the cob (5 medium ears) or 2 cans of whole kernel corn (drained)

1 small green pepper, finely chopped

1 teaspoon paprika

1/4 cup light cream

3 tablespoons cooking oil

1 teaspoon onion salt

1/2 teaspoon pepper

Combine ingredients. Spread in heavy skillet. Place over medium heat. Cook until browned on bottom, if from a can, and keep moving around in skillet to even cook. Reduce heat to very low. Cook cob corn until it is soft and tender, also moving around in skillet to evenly cook.

Good Potato Pancakes:

This is a good one for leftover mashed potatoes:

Leftover mashed potatoes

1 egg

Salt and pepper to taste

Yellow onion (chopped)

1 sprinkle or 2 of flour

Oil for frying

Heat oil. Make sure it is good and hot. Mix ingredients well. Spoon balls into ready hot oil and flatten slightly. Turn when crispy on one side and then the other. Do not turn until you know it is brown because it will tear apart. Drain on paper towel.

The more potatoes you use, the more servings you'll have.

My Oh-So-Good Mashed Potatoes:

Boy, these potatoes are so good:

   Russet potatoes (desired amount)

   1 stick of butter

   2 large tablespoons of mayonnaise

   Salt to taste

   Pepper (I really add a lot of pepper. That is the secret to these wonderful potatoes.)

   Milk as desired; do not make mushy

Cut potatoes in chunks and boil for about 10 to 12 minutes. Do not let them cook too long; just until tender. Drain water. Add butter. Let melt. Whip with electric mixer and add mayonnaise, salt and pepper, and milk if desired. Whip until creamy.

Good Old Tallarene:

My husband loved this dish with a big piece of garlic bread and salad. This can be your whole meal:

2 cups elbow macaroni, boiled and drained

1 lb. ground hamburger

1 8oz can tomato sauce

1 can (15oz.) whole corn (drained)

1 medium onion, chopped

2-3 tbsp. butter

Salt (to taste)

Pepper (to taste)

Seasoning powder (to taste)

Garlic powder (to taste)

Mince and fry onion in butter until brown. Add the meat, and stir and cook until browned. Cook noodles in water until tender. Drain most of the water out. Add tomato sauce and meat mixture. Mix well. Let simmer until good and hot. Serve with garlic bread and a salad.

My Yummy Oven Fried Potatoes:

8 large, peeled baking potatoes (I use russets) cut into medium-sized pieces (or desired amount) so good mixed with a bowl of my pinto beans:

Oil (I use extra virgin olive oil)

Salt (to taste)

Pepper (to taste)

Garlic powder (to taste)

Seasoning salt (to taste)

Onion powder (to taste)

Paprika

I cut potato pieces in a bowl big enough to be able to mix good. I first sprinkle oil all over them to coat them good. Combine the rest of the ingredients to your taste. Mix well. Line a baking sheet with tin foil and spray with a cooking spray. Spread out the potatoes on the baking sheet so they are not bunched together.

Bake at 375 degrees for 45 minutes or until potatoes are golden brown and tender.

Skillet Taters:

Peel and dice about 3 potatoes and place in skillet with 1/4 cup butter. Chop coarsely about 1 1/2 to 2 cups of onions and dump in with the potatoes. Salt and pepper to taste. Fry until brown while stirring once in a while. Serve hot.

Pig's Tail Taters:

Take the number of potatoes desired and peel. Then, with potato peeler, cut in long, very thin strips. Soak strips in cold water for at least 1 hour. Dry gently with towel, trying not to break them. Fry in deep, hot oil and drain on paper towels. Serve hot.

Bakin' Taters Twice:

Bake potatoes as usual once. Cut open, but do not part halves. Scoop out middle, add butter and milk to it, and whip. Before finished whipping, add seasonings desired. Pile it back in shells, place favorite cheese on top, and bake until golden brown. Garnish top as desired and serve.

Tater Cakes:

1 quart mashed potatoes

1/2 cup sweet milk

Whites of 2 eggs

2 heaping tbsp. butter

1 teaspoon salt and pepper

2 egg yolks

Add milk, butter, salt, and pepper to the mashed potatoes and beat well. Beat the egg whites stiff and stir in. Form into patties or balls. Roll in the egg yolks and then in cracker crumbs. Fry in deep, hot oil. Brown on both sides.

Green Stuffed Peppers:

These were always a nice change for my family:

2 cups ground beef, browned

6 green peppers

2 cups cooked rice (or 1 cup bread crumbs or, if in a great hurry, 1/2 cup corn bread mix from a package)

1/4 cup chopped parsley

2 tbsp. grated onion

2 cups canned tomatoes, diced

Garlic powder (to taste)

Seasoning salt (to taste)

Pepper (to taste)

Cut off tops of peppers. Remove seeds. Preboil peppers 10 minutes. Drain. Mix together meat, rice, parsley, onion, tomatoes, and seasonings. Stuff peppers with mixture. Sprinkle with parmesan cheese.

Place in baking dish in bottom of which is a small amount of water (or tomato sauce).

Bake in moderate oven 350 degrees for 30 minutes.

Serves 6.

Hints for Desserts:

1. To make long, curled chocolate shavings for cakes, pies, or pudding. Use the vegetable peeler to shave the chocolate. This also works well for frozen butter.
2. Grating a stick of butter softens it quickly. So will a few seconds in your microwave.
3. Save colored maraschino cherry juice and spiced apple juice for cooking rice or tapioca puddings to add color and flavor.
4. Save the liquids from canned fruits and thicken them with cornstarch. Heat and serve as sauce over cake or pudding.
5. To prevent a skin from forming on top of refrigerated puddings, place transparent plastic wrap lightly over the top of the dish. Don't let wrap touch the pudding.
6. To cream butter and sugar, put them in a warm bowl and beat as usual until mixture is like whipped cream.
7. When a recipe calls for a quantity of melted butter, measure it after melting, not before.
8. When baking milk pudding, place the dish in a pan of water in the oven. This prevents the pudding form burning or boiling over.
9. Before returning an opened carton of ice cream to the freezer, press plastic wrap onto the surface of the ice cream to prevent ice crystals from forming.
10. Whipped cream can be made well in advance without separating. Sprinkle 1/2 tsp. unflavored gelatin over 1 tbsp. of cold water in a custard cup and then set

the cup over simmering water to melt the gelatin. Whip 1 cup of heavy cream until almost stiff. Add the gelatin mixture and whip until stiff. Cover and refrigerate as long as 3 days.

11. If you like whipped cream sweetened, it will be fluffier and less likely to separate when made ahead if you use confectioners' sugar instead of granulated sugar.

12. Heavy cream will whip faster if you chill the bowl and the beaters in the freezer until they are very cold.

13. Avoid using the ultra-pasteurized variety of heavy cream. It takes much longer to whip.

14. Evaporated milk has considerably less cholesterol than heavy cream and can be whipped like cream. Pour it into an ice cube tray and freeze for about 1/2 hour or until ice begins to form around the edges. Remove the tray from the freezer, pour the milk into a chilled bowl, and whip it with a chilled electric beater until it thickens.

Hints for Cakes, Frostings, and Toppings:

1. When baking cakes and quick bread in the microwave, fill the pans just half full of batter, as they rise higher than in conventional ovens.

2. Trace the bottom of the baking pan onto wax paper and cut it out. Now this can be placed in the bottom of the pan and the sides greased and floured like normal. When the cake is done, it can be inverted and the paper taken off while still warm with no sticking.

3. Use cocoa to dust baking tins so cookies and cakes won't have a floury look. Or sprinkle greased pan generously with wheat germ instead. It keeps the cake from sticking and adds nutrients.

4. To add an interesting flavor to cakes, beat 4 tbsp. of creamy peanut butter into the butter and sugar mixture. Beat in the eggs and proceed as directed.

5. Grated orange and lemon rind added to a cake mixture gives the cake a nice flavor and prevents it from becoming stale.

6. As you take a cake from the oven, place it for a very few moments on a cloth wrung out of cold water. Then it might be turned out easily without sticking to the pan.

7. The cake is done when it shrinks slightly from the sides of the pan or if it springs back when lightly touched with the finger.

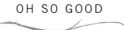

8. Always put a pan of water on the bottom shelf of oven ... that will keep your cakes very moist.

9. Spaghetti is great with cake. While waiting for icing to set, a few sticks of dry spaghetti will hold the layers in place. Also, a piece of raw spaghetti works well to light birthday candles. Try using spaghetti instead of a toothpick to check your cake for doneness.

10. If powdered sugar is sprinkled on top of each layer before filling or frosting, this will keep the filling from soaking through the cake.

11. Icing won't become grainy if a pinch of salt is added to the sugar.

12. To keep powdered sugar icing moist and prevent cracking, add a pinch of baking soda or baking powder.

13. Your frosting will look professional if you first frost with a thin layer and let it set. Then apply a second coat of frosting.

14. A quick frosting can be made by adding a bit of chocolate syrup to prepared whipped topping.

15. If icing isn't thick enough and runs down the sides of the cake, sift powdered sugar over it and the dripping will stop.

One 9-Inch Pastry Shell:

Cutting the shortening in two stages makes this all-purpose pastry both tender and flaky:

>   1 cup all-purpose flour
>
>   1/2 teaspoon salt
>
>   1/3 cup shortening
>
>   2 1/2 to 3 tbsp. cold water

Stir together flour and salt in mixing bowl. Cut in half of shortening using pastry blender or two knives until mixture is fine and mealy. Cut in remaining shortening until mixture is consistency of small peas. Sprinkle water over the mixture. Stir gently with a fork until dough leaves sides of bowl. If some dry particles remain in bottom of bowl, sprinkle with about 1/2 tsp. water. Continue to stir with fork until particles are worked into dough. Mixture should be moist enough to form a ball but should not be sticky. Shape dough into a ball. Flatten on lightly floured board. Roll into a circle about 1 inch larger than the rim of pie pan. Carefully roll dough around rolling pin. Unroll into pie pan, being careful not to stretch pastry. Fit pastry into pan, trimming 1/2 inch beyond rim. Fold overhand under and then press to form decorative edge as desired. Makes one 9-inch pastry shell

Preheat oven to 475 degrees. Prick bottom of crust thoroughly with fork that has been dipped in flour. Bake 8-10 minutes or until light brown. Cool.

Pastry for Two-Crust Pie:

2 cups sifted all-purpose flour

1 tsp. salt

2/3 cup shortening

4 1/2 to 5 tbsp. cold water

Stir together flour and salt in mixing bowl. Cut in half of shortening using pastry blender or two knives until mixture is fine and mealy. Cut in remaining shortening until mixture is consistency of small peas. Sprinkle water over the mixture. Stir gently with a fork until dough leaves sides of bowl. If some dry particles remain in bottom of bowl, sprinkle with about 1/2 tsp. water. Continue to stir with fork until particles are worked into dough. Mixture should be moist enough to form a ball but should not be sticky. Divide dough in half. Shape first half of dough into a ball. Flatten on lightly floured board. Roll into circle about one inch larger than rim of pie pan. Carefully roll dough around rolling pin. Unroll into pie pan, being careful not to stretch pastry. Fit pastry into pan, trimming edge even with rim of pan. For top crust, repeat procedure for bottom crust, carefully placing pastry over filling. Trim edge 1/2 inch beyond rim. Fold top crust edge under bottom crust, and then press to form decorative edge as desired.

Preheat oven to 475 degrees. Bake 8-10 minutes or until light golden brown. Cool.

Apple Fritters:

1 cup flour

1 1/2 teaspoon baking powder

1/2 teaspoon salt

1 egg beaten

1/2 to 3/4 cup milk

1 tablespoon melted butter

1 tablespoon sugar

1 cup peeled and diced apples

Mix all ingredients together. Combine rest of ingredients and add to the dry mixture. Use right amount of milk to make right consistency batter. Drop by spoonful in deep, hot shortening 365-375 degrees until done, which will take five minutes. Sprinkle with powdered sugar.

Mamas Pumpkin Pie:

Could hardly wait for the holidays to get this pie:

> 3 tbsp. flour
>
> 1/2 teaspoon cinnamon
>
> 1/2 teaspoon nutmeg
>
> 2 cups canned pumpkin
>
> 1 cup condensed milk
>
> 2 eggs
>
> 3/4 cups sugar
>
> 1/2 teaspoon salt

Separate eggs and combine yolks with all other ingredients in iron skillet. Cook over medium heat until thickened. Set off to cool. Beat the egg whites to stiff peaks, and then fold into the mixture after it has cooled to a lukewarm temperature. Pour into baked pie shell. Serve with whipped cream or plain.

Fried Apple Pies:

Everyone will think you are something special with these fried apple pies.

Make a nice, rich pastry dough. Cut in 5 or 6-inch squares. Place cooked apples, and 4 cups of sugar in and fold over. Moisten edges to make them stick together. Fry in deep fat at about 370 degrees until done. They will be puffed and brown on both sides, turning once when done. Drain on paper towels to get rid of grease.

Fried Peach Pies:

Combine 5 cups dried peaches, 4 cups sugar, and water to cover. Cook down until tender. Mash peaches with potato masher, add sugar, and let cool.

Use a good pastry dough for the crust. Homemade is best. Cut the dough about 5 to 8 inches. Place about 1/4 cup peaches in each crust, fold over, (turn over like a turnover) and stick edges of crust together. You might have to dampen the edges to get them to stick good. Fry until brown, turning one on each side, in well-greased skillet.

Apple Crisp:

2 cups oatmeal

1 cup brown sugar

1 1/4 cup flour

3/4 cup butter

3-4 Sliced apples

1tsp. Cinnamon

Syrup ingredients:

1 1/2 cup white sugar

3 tbsp. cornstarch

1 1/2 cups water

Mix oatmeal, brown sugar, flour, and butter together. Pat 1/2 of the mixture in bottom of greased 9x13-inch baking glass dish. Next, add sliced apples until dish is 3/4 full.

Mix syrup ingredients together and bring to a boil, allowing it to thicken. Pour syrup over apples and sprinkle generously with cinnamon. Crumble rest of crumb mixture on top. Bake 350 degrees for 50-60 minutes.

Blackberry Dumplins:

Wonderful over vanilla ice cream:

Part One:

3 pints ripe blackberries

3/4 cup water

1 cup sugar (sweetness to taste)

1 1/2 tablespoons butter

Combine in pan and let set while fixing part two.

Part Two:

2 cups flour

3 tablespoons sugar

1 teaspoon salt

1 egg

3 1/2 teaspoons baking powder

milk

Sift the flour, sugar, salt, and baking powder into mixing bowl. Add egg, mix well, and then add enough milk to make stiff batter. Now place part one on stove and bring to a boil and drop the dumpling batter a spoonful at a time into the boiling mixture. Cover with lid and cook for about 15 to 20 minutes. Can be served with cream, ice cream, or whipped cream. Can be changed by using other berries.

Apple Dumplins:

Make a rich biscuit dough, the same as soda or baking powder biscuit, only adding a little more shortening. Take a piece of dough out on the molding board, roll out almost as thin as pie crust, and then cut into square pieces large enough to cover an apple. Put two apple halves that have been pared and cored into the middle of each piece. Sprinkle on a spoonful of sugar and a pinch of ground cinnamon. Turn the ends of the dough over the apple and seal them tight.

Lay dumplings in a butter pan, the smooth side upward. When the pans are filled, put a small piece of butter on top of each, sprinkle over a large handful of sugar, turn in a cup of boiling water, and then place in a moderate oven for three quarters of an hour.

Serve with pudding sauce or cream and sugar

Vinegar Cobbler:

You have to try this one. My husband's mother made this one, and it is so good:

Part One:

1 cup sugar

2 eggs

2 tablespoons vinegar

2 tablespoons flour (or corn starch)

1 cup water

1/2 teaspoon lemon extract

Combine sugar, eggs, vinegar, flour (or corn starch), lemon extract, and water in deep pan and cook until boiling until slightly thick and smooth, stirring occasionally.

Part Two:

2 cups flour

3 tablespoons sugar

1 teaspoon salt

1 egg

3 1/2 teaspoons baking powder

milk

Sift the flour, eggs, salt, and baking powder into mixing bowl. Add egg, mix well, and then add enough milk to make stiff batter.

Drop the dumpling batter a spoonful at a time into the boiling mixture. Cover the lid and cook for about 15 or 20 minutes.

White Chocolate Cake:

This recipe makes a real scrumptious cake. It uses the summer coatings they call white chocolate:

Melt 1/4 pound white chocolate in 1/2 cup hot water. Cool.

Cream 1 cup butter and 1 cup sugar. Mix in 4 egg yolks one at a time, beating after each addition. Add white chocolate mixture and 1 teaspoon vanilla.

Sift 2 1/2 cups flour, 1 teaspoon soda, and 1 teaspoon salt and add alternately with 1 cup buttermilk. Do not overbeat. Fold in 4 stiffly beaten egg whites. Gently stir in 1 cup chopped pecans and 1 cup coconut.

Bake 25 to 30 minutes in 350-degree oven. Makes three layers.

Frosting: 1 cup condensed milk, 1 cup sugar, 4 tablespoons butter. Stir and bring to a boil. Add 3 egg yolks and 1 teaspoon vanilla. Cook approximately 15 minutes on low heat. Add 1 cup coconut and 1 cup pecans and beat until smooth and creamy.

Moms Dripping Icing:

This icing or sauce you put on after the piece of cake is served. Each person can do their own:

Combine in a small pan:

1 1/2 cups milk

1 cup sugar

2 or 3 drops vanilla

3 tablespoons flour

Dab of butter

Stir all of the time while cooking. Boil until thickened, and then it is ready to use on cake. Real good on chocolate cake.

Mom's Homemade Chocolate Cake:

This is one of my family's favorite cakes, especially with a good drippy sauce:

1 teaspoon baking soda

1/2 cup boiling water

2 heaping tablespoons cocoa

2 cups flour

2 cups sugar

1/2 cup shortening

1 teaspoon salt

2 eggs

1 teaspoon vanilla

1 cup buttermilk

Combine soda, boiling water, and cocoa. Set aside to cool. Cream together sugar and shortening. Beat in eggs. Add dry ingredients and buttermilk alternately. Stir in vanilla and chocolate mixture (chocolate should be lukewarm) and pour into a well-greased and floured glass baking dish. Bake at 350 degrees for 25 to 30 minutes.

This cake is very good warm with the dripping icing.

Old-Time Coffee Cake:

1/2 cup butter (softened)

1 cup sugar

2 eggs

1 teaspoon vanilla

2 teaspoon baking powder

2 1/4 cups flour

1/2 teaspoon salt

2/3 cup milk

Cream the butter, sugar, eggs, and vanilla. Sift together dry ingredients and add alternately with milk. Spread half of the batter into greased glass baking dish and then half of topping. Add remaining batter and topping.

Bake at 350 degrees for about 45 minutes.

Topping:

1 1/2 cup brown sugar

1 1/2 cup chopped nuts

2 tbsp. white sugar

1 tsp. flour

2 tbsp. cinnamon

Moisten with 4 tbsp. melted butter and 2 tbsp. of water.

Gingerbread:

Topped with whipped cream:

 1 cup sugar

 2 teaspoons soda

 1/2 cup molasses

 1/4 tsp. cinnamon

 1/4 tsp. nutmeg

 2 tsp. ground ginger

 2 eggs

 1/2 cup oil

 2 cups flour

 1 cup boiling water

 1/4 tsp. salt (add to flour)

Put sugar, eggs, soda, spice, and molasses in mixing bowl. Mix well, and then add shortening, flour, and last the boiling water and mix quickly. Do not mix with electric mixer, as this does not want to be beaten very much. Put into well-greased glass baking pan. Put into oven quickly.
 Bake at 350 degrees for 45 minutes.

My Favorite Peanut Butter Cookies:

I always have to make these cookies for my husband. They are one of his favorites:

    1 cup shortening

    1 cup granulated sugar

    1 1/2 cups creamy peanut butter

    1 cup brown sugar

    2 eggs

    1 tsp. vanilla

    1/4-oz. can sweetened condensed milk

    3 cups sifted flour

    2 tsp. soda

    1/8 tsp. salt

Thoroughly cream the shortening, sugars, eggs, sweetened condensed milk, and vanilla. Stir in peanut butter. Sift dry ingredients. Stir into creamed mixture.

Drop rounded teaspoons on ungreased cookie sheet. Press with back of floured fork to make a crisscross.

Bake in 350-degree oven about 10 minutes, depending on your oven. Be careful not to burn.

For richer cookies, use 2 cups of flour.

German Sweet Chocolate Cake:

This homemade cake is so good:

    1 (40-oz.) bar Baker's German Sweet Chocolate
    1/2 cup boiling water
    1 cup butter
    2 cups sugar
    4 egg yolks
    2 1/2 cups flour
    1 tsp. vanilla
    1 tsp. salt
    1 tsp. baking powder
    1 cup buttermilk
    4 egg whites, stiffly beaten

Melt chocolate in water. I put in a double boiler on the stove. Let cool. Cream butter and sugar until fluffy. Add egg yolks one at a time, beating well after each one. Add melted chocolate and vanilla. Mix well. Sift together flour, salt, and soda. Add alternately with buttermilk to chocolate mixture, beating after each addition until smooth. Fold in egg whites. Pour batter into three 8 or 9-inch layer pans, well-floured and greased. Line the bottoms with wax paper. Bake at 350 degrees for 30 to 40 minutes. Cool.

   Top with coconut pecan frosting

Coconut Pecan Frosting:

1 cup evaporated milk

1 cup sugar

3 eggs

1/2 cup butter

1 tsp. vanilla

1 cup pecans (chopped)

1 1/3 cup coconut flakes

Combine and cook over medium heat until thickened, about 12 minutes. Beat until thick enough to spread on cake.

My Good Old Sugar Cookies:

My mother and grandmother made these cookies once a week because they are so easy, and they are still the best:

    2 1/2 cups flour

    3/4 tsp. salt

    1/2 tsp. baking soda

    1/2 cup butter

    1/2 cup vegetable shortening

    2 tbsp. milk

    1 cup sugar

    1 tsp. vanilla

    14-oz. can sweetened condensed milk

    1 egg

Sift dry ingredients together and put in a separate bowl. Set aside.

Cream butter, shortening, and sugar until light and fluffy. Add egg, sweetened condensed milk, and vanilla.

Beat in dry ingredients until smooth. Blend in milk.

Drop by tablespoons about 3 inches apart onto a greased cookie sheet.

Bake 10-12 minutes in oven until lightly browned.

Makes approximately 3 doz.en cookies.

My Oh-So-Good Peanut Butter Candy:

I grew up with delicious candy my mother and grandmother made every Christmas. It was the best thing I thought we had, and Christmas was the only time it was made. A good memory:

2/3 cups peanut butter (creamy)

3 cups sugar

1/8 tsp. salt

1 1/2 cups evaporated milk

1/4 butter pat

1 tsp. vanilla

Thoroughly combine first 3 ingredients in a heavy saucepan. (I use a large skillet.) Stir in milk. Bring to a bubbling boil on medium heat, stirring constantly. Stop stirring and take the spoon out. Boil without stirring to 234 degrees (softball stage). I keep testing in a cup of water until it reaches the right ball form. Remove from heat. Add the pat of butter and vanilla. Stir. Cool at room temperature. Beat until candy thickens and loses its gloss. Quickly spread in a lightly buttered 8 or 9-inch pan.

Cool. Makes 3 dozen squares.

My Delicious Pineapple Cake:

This cake is so good I could eat it every day:

2 beaten eggs

1 20-oz. can crushed pineapple (drained)

2 1/2 cups flour

2 cups sugar

1 teaspoon vanilla

2 teaspoon soda

1/2 cup chopped nuts (more to taste)

Mix all ingredients together and pour into an ungreased 13x9-inch low glass baking dish as a sheet cake. Bake 30 to 40 minutes at 350 degrees.

Cream Cheese Frosting

1 8-oz. cream cheese (softened)

1/4 cup butter (melted)

1 teaspoon vanilla

2 cups powdered sugar

1 cup nuts (chopped)

Mix first three ingredients together until nice and creamy, and add powdered sugar and mix. Spread over cool cake. Sprinkle chopped nuts over top

My Mamas Good Persimmon Cookies:

My mother made the best persimmon cookies, so now it is my turn to achieve the best:

1 cup persimmon pulp

1 teaspoon soda

1 1/2 cups sugar

1/2 cup vegetable oil

1 egg beaten

2 cups flour (added a little at a time)

1 teaspoon cinnamon

1/2 teaspoon nutmeg

1/2 teaspoon salt

1 1/2 cups chopped nuts (more if desired)

Beat the persimmon pulp, baking soda, sugar, and oil until creamy. Add the egg, flour, spices, and nuts. (Nuts go in last.) Drop by teaspoonful on greased baking sheet.

Bake at 350 degrees for 8 to 10 minutes or until done.

Makes about 3 doz.en cookies.

My Old-Time Cocoa Fudge:

Yum! This is the only fudge I had when I was growing up, and it is still the best fudge there is. It's an oldie, but boy, it sure is good:

2 cups sugar

1 cup milk

4 tbsp. cocoa

1 tbsp. butter

Pinch salt

1 teaspoon vanilla

Grease a cookie sheet.

In a saucepan, combine the sugar, milk, cocoa, and salt. Cook to the soft ball stage, and keep checking in a cup of water until it reaches the right consistency of the ball stage. That means to drop a little bit of drippings off the spoon in to the cup of water and see if it forms into a ball. When it is just right, turn the burner off and add the butter and vanilla. Whip it and pour onto the cookie sheet and let cool.

Cut into squares.

My Spare Moment Cashew Fudge:

One day, I wanted to make fudge 'cause I was hungry for it. I was pregnant, so maybe that had something to do with it. Well, I got started and forgot I didn't have any walnuts or cocoa to put in it, only cashews and brown sugar, so that is what I used. And it is delicious:

1/2 cup butter

1 cup packed brown sugar

1/4 cup milk

1 3/4 to 2 cups sugar

1 cup cashews

Grease a 9x13-inch glass dish.

In a saucepan, melt the butter and add the brown sugar. Cook over low heat for 2 minutes, stirring constantly. Add the milk and continue cooking, stirring until the mixture boils.

Remove from heat and allow to cool.

Gradually add the confectioners' sugar until the mixture is of fudge consistency, and add the cashews. Spread in the prepared glass dish and cool. Cut into squares.

Good Old Simple Sugar Peaches:

When I have really ripe peaches, I always make this; it is so simple and easy and good:

> 2 quarts peaches or less (cut up in chunks)
> 6 cups sugar (or less)

Cut peaches in pieces and put in a large bowl, and add sugar and mix good. Cover and set in the refrigerator overnight. That way, it can make its own juice. The next day, the sugar has melted in the peaches.

Put some in separate bowls and enjoy.

Oh Yummy Sour Cream Coffee Cake:

When I was younger, I could smell this walking home from school. My mother was just taking it out of the oven:

    1 box yellow cake mix

    1 3-oz. instant vanilla pudding

    4 eggs

    1/2 cup oil

    1 cup sour cream

    1/2 cup brown sugar

    1/2 cup chopped nuts

    2 1/2 tsp. cinnamon

Mix cake mix, pudding, eggs (one at a time), oil, and sour cream. Beat 4 minutes. Grease pan (bundt or angel). Put in half of batter. Combine sugar, nuts, and cinnamon. Sprinkle this mixture on top of batter and then add remaining batter. Swirl cake with a knife and bake at 300 degrees for 50 to 55 minutes. Cool cake 10 minutes before removing from pan.

Not Halloween Pumpkin Cake:

When my sisters and myself were little, my mother used to tease us that this cake was for Halloween, and boy, we sure had it a lot and, of course, always at Halloween too:

4 eggs

2 cups sugar

1 1/2 cups oil

1 can pumpkin

2 cups flour

2 tsp. cinnamon

2 tbsp. salt

2 tsp. soda

2 tsp. baking powder

1 1/2 cups nutmeats

1 1/2 cups coconut

Beat eggs. Add sugar, oil, and pumpkin. Mix well. Add remaining ingredients to mixture. Bake in a 9x13-inch pan at 350 degrees for 40 minutes.

1/2 stick margarine (melted)

2 cups powdered sugar

1 3-oz. package cream cheese

1 tsp. vanilla

Mix ingredients together with electric mixer. Thin with milk as needed for desired consistency.

My French Strawberry Glazed Pie:

My husband always liked this pie. Of course, he liked strawberries a lot. He wasn't too crazy about cream cheese, but as long as the strawberries drowned the taste out, it was okay:

1 9-inch baked pie shell

4 cups fresh strawberries

1 8-oz. package cream cheese

1 or 2 tbsp. cream

1 cup sugar (or, to taste, I like my berries sweet)

3 tbsp. cornstarch

1/2 pt. whipping cream

Wash and clean strawberries. Blend cream cheese with enough cream to soften. Spread over the cooled pie shell. Cover with 2 cups of the choicest strawberries. Mash the remaining berries. If necessary, add water to make 1 1/2 cups. Mix sugar and cornstarch. Combine with mashed berries and cook over low heat, stirring constantly until clear and thickened. Cool. Pour over berries in the pie shell. Chill about 2 hours. Serve with sweetened whipped cream.

Delicious Lemon Bars:

We all love lemon pie, and these are just as good to the last one:

2 1/4 cups flour

1/2 cup powdered sugar

1 cup butter (melted)

4 eggs

2 cups sugar

4 tbsp. lemon juice

Combine 2 cups flour, butter, and powdered sugar and press into a 9x13-inch pan. Bake at 325 degrees for 20 minutes. For filling, beat eggs, sugar, 1/4 cups flour, and lemon juice until fluffy. Pour over baked crust and return to oven for 25 to 35 minutes. When bars are done, dust with powdered sugar. Cool well before cutting.

Googly Pumpkin Bars:

Good in season or out. Yummy:

4 eggs

1 2/3 cups sugar

1 cup vegetable oil

1 (16-oz.) can pumpkin

2 cups flour

2 tsp. baking powder

2 tsp. cinnamon

1 tsp. salt

1 tsp. baking soda

1 3-oz. package cream cheese

1/2 cup butter, softened

1 tsp. vanilla

2 cups powdered sugar

In mixer bowl, beat together eggs, granulated sugar, oil, and pumpkin until light and fluffy. Stir together flour, baking powder, cinnamon, salt, and soda. Add to pumpkin mixture and mix thoroughly. Spread batter in ungreased 15x10x1-inch baking pan. Bake in a 350-degree oven for 25 to 30 minutes. Cool. Frost with cream cheese icing. Cut in bars. Makes 2 doz.en. To make cream cheese icing, cream together cream cheese and butter. Stir in vanilla. Add powdered sugar in a little at a time, beating well until mixture is smooth.

My Mamas Easy Brownies in a Hurry:

My mama always made these in a hurry when she had to go somewhere and needed a quick dessert for after dinner:

2 cups sugar

1 stick butter (melted)

1 1/2 cups flour

1/2 cup cocoa

1/4 tsp. salt

4 eggs (beaten)

2 tsp. vanilla

1 cup nuts (chopped) (optional)

Mix well and pour into a greased 9x13-inch pan.
   Bake 25 minutes is a 350-degree oven, careful not to burn.

My Backyard Lemon Squares:

We had a big lemon tree in our backyard. All I knew when I was growing up was that lemons were only to make lemonade. So I said, "I can make something else with these," so I just added this and some of that and they become lemon squares:

3/4 cup butter (melted)

1/2 cup powdered sugar

1 1/2 cups flour

3 eggs, beaten

1 1/2 cups sugar

3 tbsp. flour

3 tbsp. lemon juice

Combine butter, powdered sugar, and 1 1/2 cups flour. Mix well and press into greased 13x9-inch pan and build up the sides. Bake at 350 degrees for 20 minutes, depending on your oven. Be careful not to burn.

While this bakes, mix eggs, sugar, remaining flour, and lemon juice. Pour over hot crust and bake 20 to 25 minutes longer, again depending on your oven.

When cool, sprinkle with sifted powdered sugar.

Oh Yummy My Piña Colada Cake:

This cake I always made on New Year's Eve, and you will want to also:

1 package yellow cake mix

1 (8-oz.) can crushed pineapple in juice, undrained

1/3 cup vegetable oil

3 eggs

1/2 cup shredded coconut

2 tsp. rum flavoring

1 (8-oz.) carton frozen whipped topping, thawed

Toasted coconut

Heat oven to 350 degrees.

Grease and flour 2 round 8 or 9x1 1/2-inch pans (or a 13x9x2-inch rectangular pan). In large mixing bowl, mix cake mix, crushed pineapple, vegetable oil, and eggs. Beat on a medium speed for 2 minutes. Stir in coconut and rum flavoring. Pour into pans.

Bake 30 to 35 minutes for round pans or 35 to 40 minutes for 9x13-inch pan.

Cool and frost cake with whipped topping. Sprinkle with toasted coconut. Refrigerate cake.

Oh Yum Peanut Butter Brownies:

Boy, these make you want more than one:

1 cup flour

1/2 tsp. salt

1 stick butter

1 cup sugar

4 eggs

1 tsp. vanilla

1 (16-oz.) can chocolate syrup

3/4 cup peanut butter

1 tbsp. melted butter

2 squares semi-sweet chocolate

1 1/2 tbsp. butter

Grease a 9x13-inch pan. I like to use a glass pan. Sift flour and salt. Beat butter, sugar, and eggs in a large bowl until light and fluffy. Stir in flour and salt until well blended. Stir in chocolate syrup until well blended and pour into pan.

Bake at 350 degrees for 25 minutes. Cool completely. Mix peanut butter with 1 tablespoon melted butter and spread over brownies.

Melt chocolate with 1 1/2 tablespoons butter and drizzle over peanut butter.

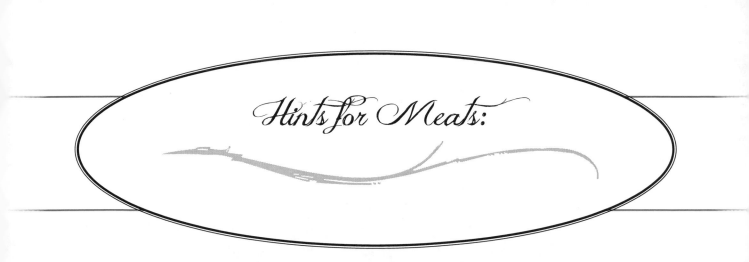

Hints for Meats:

1. Heat the frying pan before adding oil or butter to prevent sticking.

2. Sprinkle salt in the bottom of a frying pan to prevent food from sticking.

3. Try basting meatloaf with 1/2 cup brown sugar, 1 tbsp. dry mustard, 1/2 cup tomato juice, 1 1/2 cup chili sauce, and 1/2 cup pineapple juice for a delicious flavor.

4. Grate an apple into hamburger to add moistness and shape into patties.

5. A large roast or turkey can be carved easily if it stands 30 minutes.

6. To remove the wild flavor, soak game birds 3 hours in 1 tbsp. baking soda and 1 tbsp. salt to 1 gallon of water. Basting in 7-Up helps take away the game taste.

7. Add leftover coffee to ham, beef, or pork gravy for a beautiful color.

8. Use a small amount of baking powder in gravy if it seems greasy. The grease will disappear.

9. Use an ice cream dipper to make meatballs.

10. When making hamburgers, mix a little flour with the meat and they will stay together better.

11. For smooth, brown gravy, brown the flour well in meat drippings before adding the liquid. Another way to brown flour is by placing it in a custard cup beside meat in oven. When meat is done, the flour will be brown and ready to make a nice, brown gravy.

12. To prevent grease splatter while frying meat, sprinkle a little salt into the pan before putting the fat in.

13. Sausages will shrink less and not break at all if they are boiled about 8 minutes before being fried. Or you can roll them lightly in flour before frying.

14. Bacon will lie flat in pan if you prick thoroughly with a fork as it fries.

15. Bacon dipped in flour won't shrink. Pinch a fold in the middle of bacon slice to help prevent curling. Soaking in ice water a few minutes also works.

16. A quick way to separate frozen bacon: heat a spatula over the stove burner, and then slide it under each slice to separate it from the others.

17. For golden brown fried chicken, roll it in powdered milk instead of flour.

18. Try using crushed cornflakes or cornbread instead of breadcrumbs in a meatball recipe. Or use onion-flavored potato chips.

Old-Fashioned Chicken and Dumplings:

I always made these on Sundays and holidays. That was the only time they were made. But now it is whenever I get hungry for them with a plate of mashed potatoes. It doesn't get much better. Just honest country cooking. Yummy:

1 broiler fryer chicken (2 1/2 to 3 pounds)

2 quarts (8 cups) water

1 large onion, peeled and cut in half

1 tsp. salt

1/2 tsp. pepper

2 tbsp. butter

2 cups flour

1/2 cup chicken broth

1/3 cup shortening

Place chicken, water, and onion in Dutch oven. Bring to boil. Cover, reduce heat, and simmer one hour or until tender. Remove chicken from broth. Cool both chicken and broth. Bone chicken, cutting meat into bite-sized pieces. Skim fat from surface of cooled broth. Bring broth to a boil and add butter, salt, and pepper. Cut shortening into flour in mixing bowl using pastry blender or two knives until mixture resembles coarse crumbs. Add broth and stir with a fork only until dough leaves sides of bowl. Prepare your choice of dumplings.

Rolled Dumplings:

Roll out dough to 1/8 inch thickness on lightly floured board. Cut dough into strips or small squares. Slowly drop dumplings one at a time into boiling broth. Cover, reduce heat, and simmer 15 minutes or until dumplings are done. Gently stir once or twice during cooking to prevent dumplings from sticking together. Stir chicken pieces into dumplings. Let simmer

Drop Dumplings:

Pat out dough to 1/2 inch thickness on lightly floured board. Pinch off dough in small pieces. Slowly drop dumplings one at a time into boiling broth. Cover, reduce heat, and simmer 15 minutes or until dumplings are done. Gently stir once or twice during cooking to prevent dumplings from sticking together. Stir chicken pieces into dumplings and let simmer.

Chicken Breasts:

This is a good one for a fast night dinner:

  10-12 chicken breasts boned

  1 package dried beef (smoked)

  1 can cream of celery soup

  2 pints sour cream

  1 can mushroom soup

Place 1 slice of beef under each breast. Mix soups and sour cream in separate bowl. Spoon over chicken breast, covering good.

  Bake in 300-degree oven for 3 hours. Serve with rice potatoes or egg noodles.

Salmon Loaf:

I love this with a big plate of hush puppies and a nice, green salad:

 1 (16-oz.) can salmon, drained

 2 tbsp. melted butter

 1 1/2 cup soda crackers crumbs

 3 eggs

 1/2 cup milk

 salt (to taste)

 pepper (to taste)

Mix all ingredients. Add more milk if mixture is too dry. Place in greased loaf pan. Bake uncovered at 350 degrees for 25 minutes or until done.

Barbecued Pork Chops:

This is a nice change from fried pork chops:

1 tbsp. flour

1 tbsp. prepared mustard

1 tbsp. Worcestershire sauce

1/2 tsp. salt

pepper (to taste)

1/2 cup pickle juice (I use sweet pickle juice)

1/2 cup catsup

1/4 cup chopped onion

Salt meat and put in oven to heat through while mixing sauce.

Mix flour and mustard very well. Add remaining ingredients. Saturate each piece of meat in sauce and pour remaining sauce over all.

Bake at 350 degrees in covered roaster or casserole for 1 hour or until tender.

Courtney's Delicious Chicken Pot Pie:

This delicious chicken pot pie comes from my granddaughter, Courtney. The most kind, sweet, and loving person you ever want to meet. All would be very proud to call her their granddaughter. I love her dearly. You have to try this recipe. She put it together herself and it is very good:

Crust:

3 cups flour

1/2 cup butter (melted)

1 cup water

2 (8-oz.) cream cheese, softened

2/3 cup celery seed

Mix all ingredients together to form into a ball. Use half for top and the other half for the bottom. Roll half of the dough out on lightly floured board and then form on shape of pan. Bake the bottom just about 8-10 minutes, just to make sure the bottom is not a raw dough when the pie is fully done.

Filling:

In pan, heat butter to boiling and add 2 tablespoons of flour. Stir.

Add 4 cups grilled chicken (cut in pieces).

2 cups mixed vegetables

1/2 cup green onions

2 tbsp. chicken bouillon

1 tsp. salt

1/2 tsp. pepper

2-3 cups water

Mix all ingredients together and pour over bottom of crust. Roll out other half of crust and place on top of the filling. Bake in a 350-degree oven until golden brown.

My Old-Fashioned Chicken and Rice:

This is very nice for a Sunday dinner with a green salad and rolls:

2 cups uncooked rice

1-2 fryer chickens (cut up)

Pepper (to taste)

1 can chicken gumbo soup

Butter

1 package onion soup mix

1 teaspoon salt

1/4 teaspoon garlic

1 can cream of mushroom soup

3 cups water

Spread rice in a 13x9x2-inch glass baking dish. Sprinkle with 1/4 of the onion mix. Place chicken on rice. Sprinkle with remaining onion soup mix and pepper. Combine soups and water and blend. Pour over chicken. Dot with butter. Cover and bake in 325-degree oven for 2 hours.

Zuchinni Casserole:

Fast and easy for a last-minute dish:

1 lb. ground beef

4 cups sliced zucchini

1 cup mayonnaise

1 cup cheddar cheese

1 cup parmesan cheese

2 eggs

1 onion (chopped)

Salt (to taste)

Pepper (to taste)

Cook zucchini in 2 cups boiling water until tender. Brown beef and onions. Mix all ingredients together.

Pour in casserole dish. Dot with butter and cover with breadcrumbs.

Bake 1 hour at 350 degrees.

Roast Beef and Pan Gravy:

Boy this is good any day of the week. My husband, he liked his meat:

> 1 boneless beef rump roast (3 1/2 lbs.)
>
> 1 tsp. salt
>
> 1/4 tsp pepper
>
> Seasoning package (your choice) (I like Lipton's Onion Soup)

Rub roast with salt, pepper, and seasoning package fat side up on rack in roasting pan. Do not add water or cover pan. It will make its own juice.

Roast in slow oven (325 degrees) allowing 20 minutes per pound or about 1 hour and 10 minute for rare meat and 30 minutes per pound or about 1 hour and 45 minutes for medium meat.

Place roast on cutting board. Allow to stand for 15 minutes for easier carving

Beef Pan Gravy

Skim off fat from roasting pan, leaving juices. Return 1 tbsp. fat to pan and blend in 1 tbsp. flour. Cook, stirring just until mixture bubbles. Stir in 1 cup water slowly. Continue cooking and stirring, scraping baked-on juices from bottom of pan until gravy thickens and bubbles. Add more salt if needed.

Country Fried Steak with Pan Gravy:

This is always called good eating. Yummy:

6 cube steaks

2 eggs

2 tbsp. water

1/3 cup flour

1/3 cup cornmeal

1 tsp. salt

1/2 tsp. pepper

Flour (One half Pie Plate, more if needed)

Vegetable oil

Beat eggs and water together in pie plate. Mix flour, cornmeal, salt, and pepper in bowl. Dip steaks first in plain flour and then in egg mixture. Dip in seasoned flour mixture to coat well.

Brown meat 3 pieces at a time in hot oil on both sides in a large, heavy skillet. Return all meat to skillet. Lower heat. Cover. Cook 20 minutes or until tender. Remove steaks to plate.

Pan Gravy:

Pour off all but 3 tablespoons of drippings. Blend in flour. Stir in milk and salt and pepper. Continue cooking and stirring until gravy thickens and bubbles. If gravy is too thick, add more milk.

Cube Steak Haystacks:

These are always good for my Saturday night meal, fast and simple:

1 package hash brown

2 tbsp. shortening

6 beef cube steaks

1/2 tsp. soda

2 cups catsup

1 (4 oz.) package shredded cheddar cheese

Prepare hash browns as directed on package. Set hash browns aside.

In another large skillet, melt shortening. Place the steaks in skillet and cook over medium heat 3 or 5 minutes on each side or until brown. Take skillet from heat. Season each steak with salt and pepper. Then spread each steak with 2 tsp. catsup. Top each steak with 1/2 cup of the cooked hash browns, and then top each with 1 to 2 tbsp. shredded cheddar cheese. Return skillet to heat, cover, and cook over low heat 2 to 3 minutes or until cheese has melted.

Baked Chicken That Makes Its Own Gravy:

This is a change from everyday chicken:

    3 1/2 lb. frying chicken pieces

    1/4 cup flour

    1/4 cup melted butter

    2/3 cup (small can) evaporated milk

    1 can cream of mushroom soup

    1/2 tsp. salt

    1 cup grated American cheese

    1/8 tsp. pepper

    2 cups (1-lb. can) drained whole onions

    1/4 lb. sliced mushrooms

    Dash paprika

Cook chicken with flour. Arrange in single layer with skin down in melted butter in a 13x9x2-inch baking dish. Bake uncovered at 425 degrees for 30 minutes. Turn chicken. Bake until brown, 15 to 20 minutes. Remove from oven and reduce temperature to 325 degrees. Pour off excess fat. Add onions and mushrooms to chicken. Combine milk, soup, cheese, and salt and pepper. Pour over chicken. Sprinkle with paprika. Cover with foil. Return to oven and continue baking 15 to 20 minutes.

Macaroni and Cheese Casserole::

2 1/2 cups uncooked elbow macaroni

1 1/2 tbsp. salt

Dash pepper

2 1/4 cups milk

2 cups grated sharp cheese sauce (melted)

1/4 cup butter

1/4 cup unsifted flour

1 tsp. salt

1/2 tsp. dry mustard

3 tbsp. butter (melted)

1/2 cup packaged dry breadcrumbs

Preheat oven to 375 degrees.

In large pan, bring 4 quarts water to boiling. Add macaroni and salt. Boil rapidly, uncovered and stirring occasionally 10 minutes or until tender. Drain.

Meanwhile, make sauce. Melt butter in 2-quart saucepan. Remove from heat. Stir in flour, salt, mustard, and pepper until smooth.

Gradually add milk. Bring to boiling over medium heat, stirring constantly.

In 2-quart casserole, layer macaroni with 3/4 cup cheese. Repeat.

Pour sauce over the top. Sprinkle with rest of cheese.

Toss butter with breadcrumbs. Sprinkle over top. Bake uncovered 30 minutes or until cheese is golden.

Makes 4 to 6 servings.

Eggplant Italienne:

1 eggplant (about 2 lbs.)

1/4 cup unsifted flour

About 2/3 cups salad oil

1 can (15.5-oz.) spaghetti sauce with meat

1/2 cup grated parmesan cheese

Preheat oven to 375 degrees.

Wash eggplant. Cut across into 1/4-inch thick. Roll in flour.

In a little hot oil in a large skillet, sauté eggplant slices, a few browned on each side.

Layer half the eggplant slices in bottom of a 2-quart casserole. Sprinkle with half the grated cheese. Repeat layering ending with cheese.

Bake 25 to 30 minutes or until eggplant is tender and cheese is bubbly.

Makes 4 servings.

Quick Company Chicken:

1 package frozen peas or French-style green beans

2 game hens, cleaned

1 can (10.5-oz.) condensed cream of chicken soup, undiluted

1/3 cup milk

Few sprigs parsley, chopped

1/4 teaspoon sage

dash pepper

2 tbsp. sliced almonds

1 tsp. butter

1/4 tsp. salt

Preheat oven to 350 degrees.

Cut frozen vegetables block diagonally in quarters and arrange in a deep casserole dish.

Place chicken over vegetable chunks.

Bake 30 minutes.

While chicken is baking, make sauce. Stir cream soup in small saucepan until smooth. Gradually add milk, stirring to blend evenly. Mix in parsley, sage, and pepper.

Heat gradually, stirring constantly until mixture bubbles. Remove from heat.

Spoon hot sauce over baked chicken and vegetables but don't completely cover chicken.

Cover dish with foil. Return to oven and bake 1 hour and 30 minutes longer. Turn oven to 300 degrees.

In a small skillet, brown almonds in butter and salt.

Remove foil from casserole and sprinkle on almonds. Return to oven just to crisp up.

Hamburger and Noodle Stroganoff:

I remember this one when I lived at home:

 1/2 package (8-oz. size) egg noodles

 1/4 cup butter

 1/2 cup finely chopped onion

 1 clove garlic finely chopped

 1/2 lb. mushrooms, thickly sliced

 1 pound ground chuck

 1 tbsp. flour

 1 can (8-oz.) tomato sauce

 1 can (10.5-oz.) condensed beef bouillon, undiluted

 1 teaspoon salt

 1/4 teaspoon pepper

 1 cup sour cream

 1/2 cup grated parmesan cheese

 Preheat oven to 375 degrees.

Cook noodles. I cook in beef broth so you will need two cans. If I have to add water, then I do cover the noodles.

 Meanwhile, I warm butter in large skillet and sauté onion, garlic, and mushrooms until onion is golden.

 Add beef, searing until beef is browned.

 Remove from heat. Stir in flour, tomato sauce, bouillon, and salt and pepper.

Simmer 10 minutes, stirring occasionally. Blend in sour cream.

In lightly greased 2-quart casserole, layer a third of the noodles and then a third of the meat mixture. Repeat twice. Sprinkle with cheese.

Bake uncovered 25 minutes. Makes 6 servings.

Hopping Johns:

1 cup dried black-eyed peas

1/2 cup rice

end of a ham

Wash and drain peas with fresh water. Cook peas with ham bone and any bits of leftover ham until tender. Remove ham bone and separate all bits of meat. Return meat to peas and rice. Cook with sufficient water to keep mixture from sticking. When rice is tender, salt to taste. Turn heat very low and steam for 30 minutes.

Easy Shepherd's Pie:

2 packets (4 serving size) mashed potatoes (If I have mashed potatoes left over from dinner one night, I use them.)

1 tbsp. grated onion

1 egg slightly beaten

2 cups cooked hamburger

3 tbsp. finely chopped parsley

1/2 cup finely chopped celery

1 can (6-oz.) mushroom stems and pieces, finely chopped

1 1/2 tsp. salt

1/4 tsp. pepper

1/3 cup hot milk

2 tbsp. grated parmesan cheese

2 tbsp. butter

Prepare mashed potatoes according to package directions, adding grated onions to hot water required for potatoes. Beat in egg.

In a bowl, mix beef, 2 tbsp. parsley, celery, mushrooms, salt, pepper, and milk.

Preheat oven to 400 degrees. Grease a 2-quart casserole dish.

Spoon half the potato mixture (about 2 cups) into bottom of casserole. Cover with meat, and top evenly with remaining potatoes.

Sprinkle with cheese and remaining parsley. Dot with butter.

Bake 20 to 25 minutes or until surface is golden brown.

Makes 6 servings.

Baked Zucchini with Prosciutto:

3 slices prosciutto (Italian ham), diced fine

3 slices raw bacon, minced

3 tbsp. chopped parsley

1/2 medium onion, minced

Dash of black pepper

Cook 2 lbs. peeled or unpeeled 5-inch-long zucchini in boiling salted water for 3 minutes. Drain. Slice in half lengthwise. Place in single layer in greased baking dish. Sprinkle with 1/2 tsp. salt. Mix together.

Mix rest of ingredients together except for butter.

Cover zucchini halves with mixture. Pour 1/4 cup melted butter over all.

Bake in 350-degree oven for 30 to 45 minutes.

Serves 4 to 6.

Beer-Battered Fish:

This really gives it a yummy flavor:

> 2 egg yolks
>
> 1/2 cup beer
>
> 1 cup flour
>
> 1/2 tsp. baking powder
>
> 1/4 tsp. salt
>
> 1/4 tsp. pepper

Add beaten egg yolks to beer, mix together, and beat in dry ingredients. Set aside for 1/2 hour. Dip dressed fish in batter and deep fry until golden brown. Also can be friend in a hot cast-iron skillet with oil.

More beer may be added for a thinner batter.

My Easy, Fool Proof Pot Roast:

My mother told me that this was the easiest pot roast to make. This is when I first got married, and it is really good and easy:

 3 lb. pot roast

 1 package dry mushroom soup mix

 1 package dry onion soup mix

 Salt and pepper (to taste)

Sprinkle half of each soup mix on a large, heavy sheet of aluminum foil. Place roast on soup mixture and sprinkle remaining soup mixtures on top. Wrap foil securely around meat. Place in shallow baking pan. Bake at 250 degrees for 3 1/2 to 4 hours or all afternoon. Should yield lots of good gravy from drippings from meat.

My Savory Pot Roast with Harvest Vegetables:

Pot roast, good out of the oven and for leftovers:

2 tbsp. vegetable oil

3 lbs. boneless beef bottom round roast

1 can (14-oz.) seasoned beef broth

3/4 cup V8 vegetable juice

2 cups fresh baby carrots

3 medium potatoes (quartered)

3 stalks celery, cut into 1-inch pieces or smaller

1/4 cup water

Heat oil in Dutch oven. Add the roast and cook until browned on all sides. Pour off fat. Add broth and vegetable juice. Heat to a boil. Cover and cook over low heat for 1 hour and 45 minutes. Add vegetables. Cover and cook 30 minutes or until vegetables are tender. Remove roast and vegetables and keep warm.

Gravy:

Pour most of the liquid out of the roast if there is quite a bit from the cooking. That has all the spices from the meat and seasonings. If there is a lot, put it in a glass and use that. Add 2-3 table-spoons of flour to the liquid in the pan, cook, and stir. Don't let it burn. Add the liquid you saved in the glass and slowly until it starts to thicken to your desire. Turn heat off and pour into bowl.

Goodie Salmon Cakes Fried:

These are so good when they are fried crisp. My husband didn't know what these were when I first made them for him. Now I have to make them all the time:

1 to 2 (14-oz.) can pink salmon (drained and boned)

1 pack Lipton Onion dry soup mix

10 crackers (crumbled very good)

3 to 4 tablespoons good mayonnaise (more if needed)

Seasoning salt (sprinkle)

Pepper

1 egg

Sprinkle flour

1 can cream of chicken soup

Oil for frying

Mix all together except for oil. Drop by teaspoonful in hot oil in frying skillet. Smash down. Do not crowd patties. Brown on one side. Make sure it is brown before you try to turn it. Flip to other side and brown. Drain on paper towel.

Beer-Battered Fried Zucchini:

This is one of my husband's favorites:

zucchini (2-4) cut into thin slices

2/3 can beer

1 cup flour

Salt (to taste)

Pepper (to taste)

1 egg white (beaten)   Mix beer, flour, and salt and pepper in bowl. When mixed, cover and sit in the refrigerator to chill. It's best to make in the morning and let it sit all day, chilling, to use that evening. It will be thick. Stir it really good to bring it back to its original state. Add whipped egg white. Add thin-sliced zucchini. Dip each slice in batter and put in hot grease for frying. Let one side get golden brown before turning over to brown on the other side. Drain on paper towel.

Pork and Beans with Hamburger:

The first time I tasted this dish was when I started going out with my husband and his mother made it. It was so good. Now I make it all the time:

    1 large can pork and beans (1 lb. 13 oz.)

    1 lb. ground hamburger

    1 to 2 tbsp (to taste) BBQ sauce

    Big pinch brown sugar

    Onion (chopped)

Brown onions just a little in skillet, add hamburger, and cook until pink is gone. Put pork and beans, juice and all (but take out the piece of fat that comes in the can), in a bowl. Add the cooked hamburger, BBQ sauce, and brown sugar. Mix well. Transfer to deep glass casserole dish. Put in 350-degree oven until you see it bubbling and hot.

Serves 4 - 5.

Good and Yummy Rice Pilaf:

Rice is always good, plain or with butter, or with milk and sugar, or seasoned like this pilaf:

1 cup long grain white rice

1/2 vermicelli

1 cube butter (more if needed)

3 cups chicken broth

1 package Lipton Onion Soup mix

Salt and pepper to taste

Melt butter in shallow pan. Break vermicelli into bite-sized pieces and fry in butter until slightly browned, stirring constantly. Add rice to vermicelli and sauté them together for a few minutes, always stirring. Then add boiling broth, salt, pepper to taste, soup mix, stir well. When boiling, cover and put burner on low. Cook for 20 minutes or until broth is all absorbed and rice is tender. Take off fire and let rest for about 1/2 hour before serving.

Potato and Hamburger Casserole:

2 large russet potatoes

1 lb. hamburger

1/2 small bell pepper

1/2 small onion (diced)

1 can cream of celery or cream of chicken soup

1/2 can evaporated milk

salt and pepper (to taste)

2 pats of butter

Cut potatoes in small pieces and boil for 5 minutes only. Remove from heat and drain. Cook hamburger and add bell pepper and onion in skillet until medium done. Heat soup, milk, and butter. Pour over potatoes and bake in 300-degree oven for 45 minutes or until bubbling.

Serves 2 to 3.

Good Old Fried Potatoes with Onion:

The first time I tasted these, my sister made a big pan full, and they are good.

Russet potatoes, cut into thin small chunk (amount desired)

Yellow onion (chopped) 2 to 3 whole slices

Salt (to taste)

Pepper (to taste)

Oil for frying

Add all to hot oil in frying pan, turning over frequently so as not to burn. Good when good and crunchy.

Scalloped Potatoes and Pork Chops:

This is a good one. You can use pork chops or chicken:

    1/4 cup melted butter

    1/4 cup water

    4 lean pork chops

    1/4 cup dry onion soup mix

    1 tsp. salt

    8 medium potatoes, peeled and sliced thin

Put water in bottom of casserole dish and combine butter and onion soup. Layer potatoes and rest of onion soup mix 3 times. Cover with pork chops. Salt and pepper to taste. Cover and bake 1 hour at 350 degrees.
    Serves 4.

So Good Chicken and Soup Rice:

We always liked this dish when there wasn't anything else to fix. And, of course, we always had chicken:

1 chicken, cup up in parts

1 cup uncooked rice

1 (10-oz.) can cream of chicken soup

1 (10-oz.) can cream of celery soup

1 (10-oz.) can cream of mushroom soup

1 (10-oz.) can chicken broth (bouillon)

1 tbsp. sugar

Garlic salt to taste

2 tbsp. lemon juice

1/2 stick butter, melted

Dash of paprika

Combine soups, broth, and rice in a 9x13-inch pan. Mix in sugar, garlic salt, and lemon juice. Place chicken on top and drizzle butter over top. Sprinkle with paprika and bake at 350 degrees for 1 1/2 hours.

Serves 3 to 4.

My Lazy Chicken Crunch:

My husband always said, "You must have had a lazy day," because this is the dish I always make when I'm in a lazy mood that day ;

   1 can cream of mushroom soup

   1/4 cup milk

   1 cup croutons crushed

   1 tbsp. chopped onion

   1 tbsp. chopped parsley

   2 lbs. chicken parts

   2 tbsp. melted butter

   Salt and pepper to taste

Mix 1/3 cup soup, 1/4 cup milk, onion, and parsley. Dip chicken in soup mixture and then roll in croutons. Place in shallow baking dish or cookie sheet. Drizzle butter on chicken. Bake at 400 degrees for 1 hour. Meanwhile, combine the soup and milk and bring to a boil over medium heat, stirring occasionally and serve over chicken.

   Serves 3 to 4.

My Cheesy Parmesan Chicken:

I always liked this dish because when I was working it was fast and easy:

4 chicken breasts, split (and slightly tenderize between two pieces of waxed paper)

1 stick margarine

1 cup dried breadcrumbs

1/2 cup parmesan cheese

3 tbsp. chopped parsley, dried

2 tsp. salt

1/2 tsp. thyme

1/2 tsp. pepper

Garlic powder to taste

Set chicken aside. Melt butter in pan. Add to flat pie pan for dipping chicken. In separate bowl, combine crumbs and seasonings. Dip chicken in margarine. Roll in bread crumb mixture. Bake uncovered, skin side up, at 350 degrees for 1 1/2 hours. Turn over 1/2 hour before done and baste and finish cooking.

My Corny Goulash:

This is a favorite of mine when I'm at home. I hope you will try it:

    1 1/4 to 2 lb. ground beef

    2 medium onions, minced

    1 32-oz. jar Ragu spaghetti sauce

    1 can whole kernel corn (drained)

    1 cup uncooked elbow macaroni

    1/2 lb. mozzarella cheese

Brown meat and onions in skillet. Pour off grease. Cook macaroni in salted and peppered water for 8 minutes. Drain. Add meat, onions, macaroni, and corn to spaghetti sauce in a 2-quart casserole dish. Bake at 325 degrees for 30 to 45 minutes. Spread sliced or grated cheese on top and return to oven until melted.

Country Fried Steak:

If you happen to get to the general store on Saturday and they have fresh beef on hand, this is a good way of fixin' it.

To each pound of round steak, use 1 teaspoon salt, 1/4 cup flour, 1 tablespoon fat, and 1/2 cup water. Cut steak into pieces. Salt and roll in flour, and then brown in fat in large skillet. Add water, cover, and simmer until meat is tender.

The drippings in the skillet will make a mighty good milk gravy for your hot biscuits.

Milk Gravy:

Use drippings from meat. Add 2 tablespoons flour. Brown a little. Add sweet milk 1/2 to 3/4 full of skillet, salt and pepper to taste, stirring often, and let thicken to how thick you want it.

Yummy! Tamale Pie:

My mother always made this:

1 lb. hamburger

1 medium onion (chopped)

2 cloves garlic (diced)

1/2 green bell pepper

1 can tomatoes (12 oz.)

1 can whole corn (15 oz.)

1 cup cornmeal

1 7-oz. can pitted black olives

2 tbsp. chili powder (more if you like it hot)

Seasoning salt (to taste)

Pepper (to taste)

Chop onions, garlic, and pepper. Fry in oil or fat until light brown, making sure not to burn. Remove from skillet. Brown the hamburger and then combine with above. Heat tomatoes in a double boiler. When hot, stir in cornmeal. Mix well and add corn. Then add the meat mixture. Add chili powder and olives. Pour into greased casserole dish. Heat in medium oven 350 degrees for 20 minutes or until it is good and hot. Can be made ahead of time and refrigerated. Allow extra time for heating if cold.

Serves 6. Excellent for luncheon with green salad and hot rolls.

Enchilada Casserole:

This is so much easier than making a full pan of enchiladas, and it's faster:

1 lb. ground beef

1 medium chopped onion

1 can hot chili sauce

1 1/2 tbsp. flour

2 tsp. salt

1/4 tsp. pepper

1 enchilada seasoning packet

1 tsp. chili powder

1 can (4 1/2 oz.) sliced olives

6 tortillas (flour or corn; flour works best)

1 1/2 oz. cup grated cheddar cheese

Brown onion and meat. Combine sauce, water, flour, and seasoning package. Mix well. Put mixture and grated cheese between each layer of tortillas. You will finish off with meat mixture, cheese soup, and olives on top.

Bake in 400-degree oven for 35-45 minutes.